MW00577369

'Bishop Stephen's wisdom, experience and love of Jesus will nourish and encourage everyone, from new ordinands to longstanding bishops. A blessing to all those who are called to the vocation of priesthood and the service of Christ.'

The Most Revd Justin Welby, Archbishop of Canterbury

'This is an important and timely book. Bishop Stephen brings together firm biblical grounding, theological thoroughness and a "feet firmly on the ground" approach to his exploration of what it means to be a priest. It is a powerful, profound and enjoyable book that will be an invaluable resource for priests, those discerning a call to priesthood and indeed for the whole Church.'

The Rt Revd Dr Emma Ineson, Bishop of Penrith

'This book is a gem – the fruit of years of reflection on the priestly life by someone who knows its joys and temptations inside out. It will enlighten those wondering whether God is calling them to this, and inspire those who have been priests for many years and need fresh insight into the shape and character of this way of life.'

The Rt Revd Dr Graham Tomlin, Bishop of Kensington,
President, St Mellitus College

'I feel like I have been waiting for ages for this book! In a Church that is losing confidence in the language of priesthood, it is a pure pleasure to find a book that is so clear and joyful about the priestly life and yet upholds the centrality of the ministry of the baptised. This book, steeped not just in the Scriptures but in the liturgical traditions of the Church and drawing richly on years of pastoral experience, is essential reading for those exploring priesthood and indeed for all who want to understand the Church of which they are a part.'

The Rt Revd Philip North, Bishop of Burnley

'As with all Stephen Cottrell's books, this one is warm, lively and profound. Nourished by Scripture and in dialogue with the Ordinal, he offers a wealth of insights to inform and inspire those exploring ordained ministry, and to nourish and enrich the ministries of those who are ordained.'

The Revd Dr Sean Doherty, Principal, Trinity College, Bristol

'Stephen Cottrell has given us a characteristically cogent and challenging response to the questions *why priests?* and *how do we understand ordained priesthood when ministry belongs to everyone?* Weaving together Scripture, the Church's tradition, and his and others' experience of priesthood with a good dose of sound reason, Stephen gives us solid answers to affirm the nature of ordained priesthood and the threefold order of ministry, in the life of the whole people of God rooted in Christ. With his personal reflections on staying close to the cross and lives centred on prayer, Stephen has given us a powerful account that will inspire, clarify and encourage both lay Christians and the ordained, the seasoned priest and the newest ordinand alike.'

The Rt Revd Martin Seeley, Bishop of St Edmundsbury and Ipswich, Chair of the Ministry Council of the Church of England

'The Church needs ministers who know what they are called to be as well as what they are called to do. This book brings to life some familiar (and unfamiliar) biblical images of ministry and offers practical and timely words of wisdom and hope to new and experienced clergy alike.'

The Revd Dr Philip Plyming, Warden, Cranmer Hall, St John's College, Durham

ON PRIESTHOOD

Servants, Shepherds, Messengers,
Sentinels and Stewards

STEPHEN COTTRELL

HODDER &
STOUGHTON

First published in Great Britain in 2020 by Hodder & Stoughton
An Hachette UK company

4

Copyright © Stephen Cottrell, 2020

The right of Stephen Cottrell to be identified as the Author
of the Work has been asserted by him in accordance with the
Copyright, Designs and Patents Act 1988.

Scripture quotations are taken from the New Revised Standard Version Bible:
Anglicised Edition, copyright © 1989, 1995 National Council
of the Churches of Christ in the United States of America.
Used by permission. All rights reserved worldwide.

A CIP catalogue record for this title is available from the British Library

Hardback ISBN 978 1 529 36098 1
eBook ISBN 978 1 529 36100 1

Typeset in Sabon MT 11/14 pt by
Palimpsest Book Production Limited, Falkirk, Stirlingshire

Printed and bound in Great Britain by Clays Ltd, Elcograf S.p.A.

Hodder & Stoughton policy is to use papers that are natural, renewable and
recyclable products and made from wood grown in sustainable forests.
The logging and manufacturing processes are expected to conform to
the environmental regulations of the country of origin.

Hodder & Stoughton Ltd
Carmelite House
50 Victoria Embankment
London EC4Y 0DZ

www.hodderfaith.com

To all those I have had the privilege of ordaining as deacon and priest in the Reading episcopal area of the Diocese of Oxford and in the Diocese of Chelmsford – may God continue to bless and sustain you in the ministry we share.

How beautiful on the mountains
    Are the feet of the messenger who announces peace,
who brings good news
    who announces salvation,
    who says to Zion, 'Your God reigns.'
Listen! Your sentinels lift up their voices,
    together they sing for joy.

ISAIAH 52.7–8, NRSV

CONTENTS

INTRODUCTION

A friend of mine once said that the main problem with the Church was the clergy. Not the clergy as people; they were, as far as she could gather, good and honourable men and women. Well, most of them! No, it was the very *notion* of clergy that was the problem. After all, wasn't ministry supposed to belong to everyone? Wasn't this the radical idea at the heart of the New Testament?

According to her analysis, priesthood was an Old Testament idea that was done away with on the cross along with temples and sacrifices and all the other (now redundant) paraphernalia of priesthood. By bringing it back, the Church had sold out on what was essential to its vocation, to be itself the priestly people of God, exercising what she referred to as 'the priesthood of all believers'.

I've been a bishop in the Church of England for fifteen years. I have interviewed a lot of people who are seriously considering a vocation to ordained ministry. I have told this story of my friend's view of priesthood to virtually all of them. I have asked them how they would respond. Why do we have priests? And if we do have them, in the light of what we know God has done in Christ, the High Priest and perfecter of our faith, what sort of ministers should these priests be?

People's answers have varied enormously. Some, alarmingly, given that this is an interview about becoming a priest, don't seem to have given the matter very much thought at all.

Others, thinking my friend's views must also be my own, agree with her rather too readily. But most, in my view, seem too quick to go in one of two equally dubious directions. Seizing upon the two biblical passages that most readily appear to counter my friend's argument (Jesus selecting twelve apostles and then those apostles selecting seven deacons), the priesthood is either elevated to a position of grandiose leadership, or reduced to become not much more than a supervisor or manager, a keeper of the ministerial rota and the caretaker of the church.

Actually, these two pieces of Scripture *are* the key to understanding ordained ministry, but they need to be held together in creative tension, not seen as separate pathways. But that is to jump ahead of ourselves.

This book is my answer to my own question. It attempts to deal with the question: Why priests exactly, and how we should understand the ministry of the ordained priesthood in a Church where ministry does indeed belong to everyone?

As well as interviewing a lot of would-be priests, I have also ordained several hundred. It is the particular joy of episcopal ministry to be the one who ordains and sends out new ministers. Almost all the chapters in this book began life as an address given in the Chelmsford Diocesan Retreat House at Pleshey to those about to be ordained as priests in the Church of God. When I became Bishop of Chelmsford in 2010, I consciously decided to take a different aspect of ordained ministry and reflect upon it each year with those I would be ordaining the next day. These addresses are now gathered together, hacked about a bit, added to and subtracted from (I inevitably found myself saying some things every year to each group of ordinands) and brought together as what I believe is a much-needed (and, with hope, confident) re-presentation of the call to priesthood. I have edited only where necessary, either to expand a point, delete too many unnecessary repetitions from year to year (though I think the repetitions are not insignificant and therefore some remain), and then to add in some things that I believe are important, but may be not best said on the night before an ordination. But even though they have been carefully edited and woven into a book about ordained ministry, I trust that their integrity as actual addresses given to real people about to be ordained remains; and because they were always conceived as a series of addresses that would become a book, I hope readers will find that they hang together as a single enterprise, and not just a series of separate reflections.

I want very much to say how good and how beautiful it is to serve as a priest in God's Church. I want to place this vocation within the wider vocation of the whole people of God, and within the historic threefold pattern of ministry – bishop, priest and deacon – that the Church has inherited from its beginnings in the New Testament and in the first centuries of its life. I believe there is wisdom here that we neglect at our peril. It gives us a leadership and a ministry that is more than, and different from, the leadership of the world: a leadership and a ministry that is rooted in Christ.

But I also passionately believe that ministry does belong to everyone and that because of our baptism everyone has a share in the ministry of Christ and a responsibility to live as his disciples. However, I also believe that the incarnational and sacramental pattern of the Christian faith means that as Christ himself is the sacrament of God, God made visible and tangible to us in flesh and blood like ours, then it is Christ himself who ordains and sends out particular ministers, not just to lead and serve his Church (though, as we shall see, this is a primary part of ordained ministry), but also as evangelists and prophets to teach and preach, to hold the powerful to account, and to speak of God's kingdom of justice and peace in a world of ever increasing confusion and hurt. This exacting and exhilarating call to priesthood needs to be reimagined and reasserted in every generation. However, it seems especially important at the moment, not just because the world is so racked by pain and rocked by indecision, or because the failures of leadership in so many walks of life leave people unsure where to put their faith beyond the transitory pleasures of their own security and material satisfaction, but because the Church itself sometimes seems to have lost confidence in its own vocation to offer a leadership that is prophetic, contemplative and sacramental, as well as professional.

The book is also, therefore, rooted in that text that should be the title deed for all ordained ministry, namely the Ordinal: the book of ordination services given by the Church to frame and understand ordained ministry and included in the Declaration of Assent of the Church of England as one of its three most significant source documents. Of course, there is wisdom to be found elsewhere – not least in the Scriptures, but also in all kinds of other sources, both secular and sacred, where other people's reflections and experiences of leadership can inform ours. The Ordinal, though, is the book that tells us what we think ordained ministry should be. It also contains the prayers that are prayed as we are ordained.

Having said that, I realise what I am considering here may appear to be limited to Anglicans, since it is the Ordinal of the Church of England that is my source and guide in all that follows. But because, as we shall discover, the Ordinal is itself deeply rooted in the Scriptures, I hope and believe

4

that this book will be of benefit to Christians of many different denominations as we discover together what it means to lead God's Church. I also note that some of the ecumenical documents on ministry affirm and promote the ideas that I am emphasising here. So although this is unapologetically a book that focuses on Anglican ministry, I believe it can be relevant and valuable to all.

'Read poems as prayers'

In his sequence of poems *Station Island*, Seamus Heaney presents us, rather beautifully, with a 'poem within a poem'. It tells the story of someone looking for a chance to start again and to salvage what has been lost in their life. In some sort of trance-like state they either remember making their confession or perhaps even go to a priest to make a confession. The priest says this:

> What came to nothing could always be replenished.
> 'Read poems as prayers,' he said, 'and for your penance
> translate me something by Juan de la Cruz.'[1]

Such a penance is rather daunting. Hollywood has it that the absolved penitent is usually given so many 'Our Fathers' and 'Hail Marys' to say. In reality a penance is more likely to be something to be offered as a sign of amendment of life that is connected in some way to the nature of the sins confessed, or something to meditate on that will aid the amendment of our lives more generally, such as a psalm or a story from the Gospels. But to translate from the Spanish a poem by John of the Cross is, by any estimation, a tall order. For Seamus Heaney it provides the pretext for the poem within the poem:

ON PRIESTHOOD

he offers a profoundly beautiful translation of one of John of the Cross's most famous poems, 'Although it is the Night'.

I like Heaney's suggestion that we can 'read poems as prayers'. So, in recent years, whenever I have been asked to lead a retreat I have encouraged the retreatants to discover their inner poet. I have shared with them a Gospel story where Jesus is asking people questions; I have then invited them to respond by writing a poem that is – as it were – their answer to Jesus. And for those who find writing poems impossibly difficult (and they usually form the majority), I have said write a prayer instead, and then let them discover for themselves that poems and prayers are, as Rowan Williams puts it, 'close cousins'.

Some of the poems written have been very beautiful, and since most of the quiet days and retreats I lead are for clergy, I have started to amass a little collection of poems by clergy reflecting on different aspects of their ministry. It seemed fitting, then, as the Word was made flesh, and as a priest is the one who is a walking sacrament of God's love and purposes in Christ, to scatter a few of these poems throughout the book. They are not necessarily great poetry. But they are keenly felt.

Most priests are wordsmiths of one sort or another. The sermon is a little work of art. Prayers are poems. So these poems reveal the vocation of those who have worked hard for many years enfleshing faith for congregations whose members are both stubborn and eager. They are not explanations of ministry. They don't tell us what ordination means. I've tried to do that in this book. But the poems do say something else; something that prose finds elusive. They start to say how it feels to be a priest, what it costs and how faith and vocation can be sustained.

I dedicate the book to all those I have had the honour and

6

privilege of ordaining within the Church of England, and especially in the wonderfully vast and diverse Diocese of Chelmsford where I serve. On all the occasions where I have spoken to those about to be ordained I have wanted to instruct and inspire them in the ways and patterns of ordained ministry; and most of all I have wanted to share its joys and the sense of adventure that comes with following Christ in this way. For me, despite its challenges and ubiquitous encounters with darkness that can often be its daily bread, the ordained life has been a liberation and a joy (it has enabled me to become more myself, for it has been the discovery of God's call on my life). It has been joy to serve and lead the people of God and to try and bring something of the light and brilliance of Christ into the dark and neglected corners of human lives and human existence. It has been a joy to see the Church flourish and grow. It has even been a joy, though often of an acutely painful kind, to sit with those who hurt and falter, and indeed with a Church that is faltering, and try to see what Christ can do and where God's love can be found and claimed. There is, in my experience, a curiosity and longing in the human heart for the things of God: it doesn't go away, though it sometimes finds succour in other places, be they helpful, neutral, frivolous or malign. Being a priest has nourished my own humanity and helped me become the person I am meant to be. It has helped me see the world as God sees it and make the world as God would have it be.

It has been a joy to share this with others. It is, after all, the only hope for the world. How could it be otherwise? The world belongs to God, and his Christ is light and life for all.

Part One

———

CHAPTER ONE

Priests for a priestly people

I exhort the elders among you to tend the flock of God
that is in your charge, exercising the oversight, not under
compulsion but willingly, as God would have you do it.

I PETER 5.1B–2

A few years ago I was interviewing a would-be ordinand and
asked him if he had read anything about the priesthood and
if so what he'd made of it. He mentioned a book that I think
is still on many reading lists, though had better at this point
remain nameless. He said he had found it interesting, at times
insightful, but it had just left him feeling exhausted. The
model of ministry it seemed to be expounding was still one
where the priest did everything, or at least maintained control
of everything. The theological starting point seemed to be,
'priest as minister, everyone else as helper', rather than the
startling biblical vision that ministry belongs to everyone and
that the priest has a particular role within the body.

I think many books on priesthood and ministry make this
mistake, though often unwittingly. The ministry of the
'priestly people of God' soon becomes the ministry of
the ordained priest, and lay ministry is reduced to filling
gaps, undertaking delegated tasks, or merely 'helping the

vicar' – because they are obviously so busy. It was this busy-ness – and the exhaustion that goes with it – that troubled this ordinand. Although there is another danger, namely when the biblical notion of the priestly people of God becomes the impressive sounding, but in my view rather less than biblical 'priesthood of all believers'. I don't find this phrase helpful. It can lead you to think that everyone is a priest. Whereas the biblical language, as we will discover, is *corporate* not individual. 1 Peter declares that God's people are 'a chosen race, a royal priesthood, a holy nation, God's own people' (1 Peter 2.9). Every one of these phrases describes us in rela-tionship to each other – a race, a nation, a priesthood – not as individuals. This is profoundly counter-cultural. Our society teaches us to define ourselves as individuals. We prize this sense of ourselves as separate from one another and as self-determining. The radical biblical idea is that we belong to each other.

So how might we approach priesthood differently? What is the role of the ordained minister? How should we under-stand the priesthood today?

Two approaches seem to dominate contemporary thinking. First, the priest becomes a sort of manager, someone charged with responsibility for organising and maintaining the ministry of everyone else within an institution. I'm not sure this is what any of us gave our lives for. Neither do I actually think, despite some clergy insisting otherwise, that this is what any of the books or papers that are accused of turning clergy into managers actually intend. But the other approach is even more dangerous. I don't know how to sum it up, but you could describe it as 'the priest who is *definitely not a manager*'. This rather sentimental model of ministry sees the priest as someone who is far too holy to dirty their hands with any management at all, let alone leadership. The priestly hands are made to pray, bless and celebrate the sacraments. Anything else is anathema. As I shall go on to explain, priesthood has never had this purely pietistic function. But it is beguiling for some, who are daunted by the challenges of being a missionary Church that engages fully with the world it serves, and a Church in which everyone ministers.

So where, then, do we turn to uncover and understand the historic vocation of the ordained minister? Well, we start with our theology of the Church.

The Church is a community, not an organisation or an institution; a community of men and women *formed* by the death and resurrection of Jesus Christ and his impact in the world, and constantly being *transformed* by the activity and outpouring of the Holy Spirit. Yes, we have organisation. Yes, we appear to be an institution and have inevitably developed many associated characteristics and functions to operate and thrive, but, fundamentally, we remain what we have always been: a body of men and women centred on Christ, and one in which ministry is shared by everyone and in which certain people are called and commissioned (we use the word 'ordained') for a specific role of oversight.

And to understand this particular role we turn, unsurprisingly, to the Ordinal. This document – the rite that is used for the ordination of every priest in the Church of England – gives us all we need to understand the depths, functions and identity of ordained ministry, though, as we shall see, this ministry is never straightforward; and since we exercise it in many different ways according to our different gifts, calling and circumstances, we often need to place one insight alongside another and discover the truth of vocation somewhere in-between.

What may come as a surprise is that the first text in the Ordinal we need to look at is not the order for priests, but that for bishops. It is the bishop's ministry that regulates and shapes the Church on earth, and, paradoxically, it is by understanding the apostolic vocation of the bishop – the one who orders and has oversight of the whole church – that you can begin to understand and inhabit the vocation of a priest within it.

Therefore, all ordination services in the Church of England, be they for bishops, priests or deacons, begins with these tremendous words:

> God calls his people to follow Christ, and forms us into a royal priesthood, a holy nation to declare the wonderful deeds of him who has called us out of darkness into his marvellous light.

> The Church is the Body of Christ, the people of God and the dwelling place of the Holy Spirit. In baptism the whole Church is summoned to witness to God's love and to work for the coming of his kingdom.[1]

This beautifully sums up our theology of the Church and our theology of ministry. In following Christ, we are enlisted in his service. And we might add: *whether we like it or not*, we are enlisted in his service. Through baptism we all become witnesses to Christ and workers for the kingdom of God. And some Christians will not like it, and some may rail against it; but there is actually no choice: ministry is the work and witness of the whole Church. Indeed, the Introduction to the Ordinal opens with a powerful and pithy phrase that sums this up: 'The ministry of the Church is the ministry of

Christ.'[2] Each person is then called to discover their part in it. This will vary according to people's different circumstances, talents, availability, personality and passions. But even if our lives end up being a very poor witness to Christ, we are witnessing nevertheless.

The task of leadership in any organisation is the wellbeing and flourishing of the organisation itself, according to its particular vocation and purpose. It is very important to appreciate this. Get your understanding of leadership wrong, and everything that follows will be wrong as well. So in the Church, the task of leadership is to serve the whole Church and build it up so that each person may discover the part they are called to play in witnessing to Christ and building the kingdom, and to be ready for the inevitable sacrifices that go with a life following Christ, and for the conflicts and persecutions that may come. Leadership in the Church is not an easy thing.

Having said that, it is also worth noting early on that you won't find the word 'leader' in the New Testament. As Nicholas Henshall has observed, it only starts being used by the Church in the mid- to late twentieth century. He suggests we might be embarrassed by many of the traditional words the Church has used. Hopefully this won't be the case after you have read this book! But he also points out that it might be because we want to look like other organisations. Reflecting on passages such as Matthew 20.20–8, Mark 10.35–45, and Luke 22.24–7 (ones we will refer to later), Henshall writes that 'Jesus uses a whole range of words for leadership, power and authority and then explicitly and emphatically rejects them as titles for ordained elders in the Christian community.'[3] 'It will not be so among you', says Jesus (Matthew 20.26). In other words, it is not that leadership is not needed in the

Christian community, but it will be of a different type and character. It is godly, servant leadership that is required.

This might also be the point to mention that the word 'priest' isn't used in the New Testament to describe these leaders either. There was a perfectly good and well-known Greek word for priest – *hiereus* – that the New Testament writers could have used. But this is shunned as well. In the New Testament the words 'priest' and 'priesthood' are only used to describe Jesus our High Priest (see Hebrews 7.26 and 8.1) and, as we have already noted, in 1 Peter, the priesthood of the whole Church. The words the New Testament does use are *episcopos* ('over-seer') from where we get the word 'bishop', and *presbuteros*, of which the best translation is probably 'elder' but whose ideas lie behind what we now call a priest. Note in the Ordinal that the Ordination Service itself is therefore called the Ordination of Priests *also called Presbyters* (my italics).[4]

So why do we use the word 'priest'? Partly, the answer is tradition. The word 'priest' has become the default word. However, by including alongside it and in part qualifying it by saying 'also called presbyter' the Church of England makes clear that it understands a priest to be someone who by their oversight and leadership in the Church serves the priesthood of the whole people of God. This word will still be problematic for some – and priests are free to call themselves presbyters – while reassuring and irritating ecumenical partners in equal measure. Some use this word. Others definitely don't!

However, the way the word is used in the Anglican tradition, and particularly the way the meaning is fleshed out by the other words and images that the Ordinal draws from Scripture, gives us a distinct Anglican picture of what servant, priestly leadership is like, a leadership that serves the priestly ministry of the whole Church.

Therefore, the Ordinal goes on to say in each service, be it the ordination of a bishop, priest or deacon: 'To serve this royal priesthood, God has given particular ministries.'[5] For the episcopate it reads: 'Bishops are ordained to be shepherds of Christ's flock and guardians of the faith of the apostles, proclaiming the gospel of God's kingdom and leading his people in mission.[6] (We will return to the significance of the word 'shepherd' later.) As leader in mission, the bishop is ordained to teach the faith; lead the people of God in prayer and praise; train, equip, encourage, license and commission new ministers, so that the Church can become what it is meant to be, God's transforming presence in and for the world.

When a priest is licensed or instituted to lead a church (the technical word for this is that they become the incumbent of a parish), as the licence is read out and given to the priest, the bishop declares: 'Receive the cure of souls which is yours and mine'. This, too, is significant. It dramatically signifies that the mission of the Church – the care of the souls of that parish – and it must be noted it is *parish*, i.e. everyone who lives in that locality, not *congregation* – is shared by the bishop and the priest who is the bishop's representative in the parish extending their ministry of oversight, pastoral care and leadership in mission.

This, then, is the primary focus of the priest's ministry: to embody and live out the apostolic ministry – the ministry of Christ – that they share with and receive from the bishop. This is why for priests the Introduction says that they 'share with the bishop in the oversight of the Church'.[7]

It also goes on to say that 'with the Bishop and their fellow presbyters, they are to sustain the community of the faithful by the ministry of word and sacrament, that we all may grow into the fullness of Christ and be a living sacrifice acceptable to God'.[8] This again links the ministry of priest and bishop, and emphasises the purpose of this ministry which is to enable the whole people of God to fulfil their vocation to grow into the fullness of Christ and witness to God's kingdom in the world. It also says that it is by word and sacrament more than anything else that this work will be done. It is by receiving the Word of God as a light for the pathway through life (see Psalm 119.105) and the sacraments as rations for the journey, that the whole of life is rooted and shaped by Christ, and that the whole people of God are instructed and nourished and then released for their ministry in the world. This emphasis on the priest as one who works at the table and the pulpit is something we will return to again and again in this book. It is something tremendously obvious, but it is also in danger of being neglected. A priest's job is to break open God's word and to celebrate the sacraments of the New Covenant. Nothing is more basic, nor more important, for one called to priesthood and therefore to servant leadership in the Church of Jesus Christ.

But the most important text for understanding this priestly ministry is the Declaration, which is read by the bishop before the Ordination Prayer itself. This digs below the surface of the word 'priest', revealing the scriptural references and resonances that define and sustain priestly ministry in and for the Church, and starts to give us some new language.

It begins with these words:

Priests are called to be servants and shepherds among the people to whom they are sent. With their Bishop and fellow

ministers, they are to proclaim the word of the Lord and
watch for the signs of God's new creation. They are to be
messengers, sentinels and stewards of the Lord.[9]

This again emphasises how the ministry of the priest cannot
be understood apart from the ministry of the bishop; and
just as the ministry of the bishop ensures that the ministry
of the church 'in each place and time is united with the church
in every place and time'[10], so the ministry of the priest is a
continuation of this ministry, giving assurance that this local
manifestation of the one Church is also the same Church of
Jesus Christ built upon the apostles. However, in speaking
of 'fellow ministers' these opening sentences of the Declaration
also demonstrate that ministry does indeed belong to
everyone. Just as Jesus sent them out in pairs (you see, ministry
was never meant to be a solo voyage) so the ministry of the
priest cannot be understood or separated from the ministry
of the whole people of God. Thus we find these phrases later
on in the Declaration: 'With all God's people they are to tell
the story of God's love ... they are to discern and foster the
gifts of all God's people'.[11] The priest is not the one who
does all the ministry, but the one who ensures all the ministry
gets done.

The manner with which this task of leadership and oversight is undertaken is wrapped up in the five remarkably
descriptive words that also appear in these first sentences of
the Declaration and form the subtitle of this book. The priest
is called to be a servant, a shepherd, a messenger, a sentinel[12]
and a steward. These words not only flesh out the meaning
of the call to oversee the ministry of God's Church, but also
enable us to look at it from different biblical perspectives.
Even if we have only paid them scant attention, what is

interesting for ordained ministers in the Church of England is that each one of these richly biblical images has been said to every one of us. Therefore, before going any further, let us briefly examine where this Declaration and these words came from. We have already noted how important the Ordinal is for our understanding of ordained ministry. But where did the Ordinal itself come from?

The origins of the Church of England Ordinal

Every priest in the Church of England is ordained using the same ordination rite. In many respects this rite has hardly changed since Cranmer first produced it in 1550.[13] It was the one major element of the liturgy not provided in the First Prayer Book of 1549.[14]

Following the Reformation in England Thomas Cranmer set about providing a prayer book for the Church of England that would articulate its belief and doctrine through liturgy, and would therefore be its foundation and the fullest expression of its very particular trajectory which, unlike most of the other Reformation churches across Europe, was to be a national Church, i.e. a Church that was determined to be the Church for everyone. Cranmer therefore drew together the apostolic (and what we would now probably call catholic) traditions of what had gone before with the insights from the Reformers whose ideas about access to God through Christ alone were convulsing and inspiring Europe. In other words, the Reformation in England had a very particular flavour that was not quite the same as its European neighbours. The Church of England claimed to be catholic *and* reformed.

In that first Ordinal of 1550 we find the words 'messenger', 'watchman' and 'steward'. As is so often the case with liturgical texts, we might assume that Cranmer is drawing on earlier liturgical sources; actually, there is nothing quite like the Declaration, and therefore these words to describe ordained ministry do not appear in any other Ordination liturgy.

The Common Worship Ordinal of the Church of England was published in 2007. It is a reworking of the Alternative Service Book Ordinal 1980 (ASB), which is itself an adaptation of the 1662 Book of Common Prayer Ordinal.

The sentence about the priest as 'servant and shepherd' seems first to appear in the ASB in 1980, with the phrase 'you are to be messengers, watchmen and stewards of the Lord' appearing in the middle of the Declarations.[15] The Prayer Book Ordinal doesn't use the words 'servant' or 'shepherd' specifically – though there is much about being a shepherd in the rite – but the Declarations remind those being ordained of the weight of their calling, saying:

> And now again we exhort you, in the Name of our Lord
> Jesus Christ, that you have in remembrance, into how weighty
> an office and charge ye are called; that is to say, to be messengers, watchmen and stewards of the Lord.[16]

These are therefore the most ancient words for Anglicans, the ones that have been said to everybody ever ordained in the Church of England.

In producing his Ordinal, Cranmer, along with other Reformers, was reacting against some of the confusions and secondary accretions that had attached themselves to the various Roman and Gallican traditions that were in use at the time and (in his view) obscured the meaning of ordained ministry; and since Cranmer also wanted to redefine this ministry he turned to the ordination rite, *De Ordinatione Legitima*, that had been composed by the German Reformer Martin Bucer.[17] Bucer had been a master in Theological Studies in Strasbourg. Forced into exile because of the religious upheavals in Europe, he found refuge in England in 1549. He stayed as Cranmer's guest and became Regius Professor of Divinity at Cambridge, where he was to die in March 1551. Yet, 'in under two years and despite failing health, Bucer was to have a profound effect on the liturgical and doctrinal development of the Church of England'.[18] Adapting Bucer's pattern, Cranmer provided rites for the ordination of deacons, priests and bishops.

The ordination rite for deacons was the simplest – a sermon, the presentation of the candidates, the litany, the Eucharistic ministry of the word up to the end of the epistle, an examination of the ordinands, the laying on of hands by the bishop with an appropriate formula, and the giving of the New Testament.

The rite for priests was similar, except that as well as the inclusion of the ancient hymn *Veni Creator Spiritus*, there was a lengthy exhortation to the ordinands, a period of silent congregational prayer, and another substantial prayer before the laying on of hands.[19] However, these three words – messenger, watchman, steward – are Cranmer's own additions. They are not to be found in Bucer's rite, nor in any other previous or ancient rite. Although we have ancient ordination rites in the *Didache*, in the *Apostolic Tradition of Hippolytus*, and in numerous medieval rites, there is nothing like the exhortation that we find in Bucer and Cranmer. In the *Didache*, which outside of the New Testament, contains the earliest reference we have to anything like ordained ministry, those who are called to be bishops and deacons are instructed 'to perform the service of prophets and teachers'[20] The Prayer of Hippolytus uses the word 'shepherd'.[21]

It remains possible that Cranmer acquired the material from elsewhere. Surely it is fairer to suppose that it is his own composition and that the three words 'messenger', 'watchman' and 'steward' were important for his understanding of ordained ministry. The truth is, we do not know. But it is reasonable to conclude – not least because the words cannot be found anywhere else – that they are foundational and distinctive for any Anglican understanding of ordained ministry.

Moreover, emphasising the priestly vocation as that of a servant, sentinel and shepherd provides a provocative counterpoint to some of the more managerial approaches to leadership that are often assumed to downplay contemplative and prophetic aspects of Christian ministry and leadership. For this reason, if no other, it is interesting to note that no serious academic study of these words in relation to ordained ministry seems to have been written.[22] Neither have I found anything about why Cranmer used these words, nor any reference in books of liturgy, nor cross-references with the ordination rites of other churches.[23]

Of course Cranmer may not have seen the words in quite the way I'm seeing them, or as Scripture sees them. Cranmer might, for instance, have included 'watchman' on his list because he saw the ordained minister as a guardian against false doctrine rather than the prophetic voice that we find in Scripture. Following Bucer, Cranmer's own view of ordained ministry was largely utilitarian: 'there was no essential difference between having distinctive ordination rites for deacons, priests and bishops, and having distinctive royal commissions for sheriffs, justices of the peace and common law judges'.[24] Cranmer was concerned with good order. That's where the words 'ordination' and 'ordinal' come from, after all. However, in a time of massive religious and political upheaval in Europe, such an intentional strategy for including as many as possible within this new reformed and catholic national Church may itself be a consequence of Cranmer's own looking and listening as a sentinel.

In 1552 other changes were made in the Ordinal, but the Declarations remained. These words have been retained in all the revisions to the Ordinal in the Church of England ever since.

The same cannot be said for revisions of the Ordinal in the Anglican Communion. Cranmer's words have not travelled well. I have not undertaken an exhaustive study, but neither the Revised Prayer Books of Australia, Canada, New Zealand, South Africa nor the United States includes Cranmer's pithy assemblage of nouns. For instance, the Anglican Prayer Book of the Province of Southern Africa says that you are called to be a 'priest, pastor and teacher'. The Episcopal Church has something similar. Both lack the poetry and sharpness of the biblical language Cranmer employs and do not have that hinterland of meaning that invites those being ordained to unpack the word 'priest' in the light of Scripture.

I have looked at the ordination services of other denominations and cannot find anything quite like the Anglican Declaration or these words of Cranmer there either. However, this does not stop these words having the same power and relevance for Christian ministers of every church.

The first major revision to the Ordinal took place in the 1960s in what became known as Series Three, the precursor to ASB and Common Worship. A new Ordinal was approved by the General Synod of the Church of England in July 1967. Great effort was made to ensure that this text reflected growing ecumenical consensus about the nature of ordained ministry (the lack of one being a major obstacle to unity) and the interrelationship between ordained ministry and the ministry of the whole people of God.[25]

As well as the 1662 Prayer Book text, there is clear reference to the influential ordination rite from the ecumenical Church of South India[26] and the ill-fated Anglican–Methodist Ordinal.[27] But there was also discussion with the Roman Catholic Church.[28] Insisted upon by the then Archbishop of Canterbury, Michael Ramsey, this was an innovative and pioneering way of working, but also means that the text we now have, and the words about ministry we are discussing, can be said to represent a wide coming together of ideas about what ordained ministry should be.[29]

The five-stranded cord of ordained ministry

I've already mentioned the first question I ask those who see me at the beginning of their journey towards ordination. The second question, then, is always about these words. I read out the opening sentences of the Declaration from Common Worship about a priest being a servant, shepherd, messenger, sentinel and steward. I then ask them which of these words they consider the most important, and why.

Of course the correct answer is that they are all equally important. But I do not allow them the correct answer. I just invite them to select the one that seems to them to be most descriptive of the priestly vocation.

Most people opt for shepherd or servant. Some have heard that this particular bishop is keen on evangelism, so plump for messenger. Hardly anyone says steward. Only once has someone said sentinel. Yet, as you read the Ordinal, you will observe that this element of priestly ministry is vividly present in so much of the language: even in the second sentence quoted above it says that priests are to 'watch for the signs of God's new creation'. This emphasis on the priest as 'one who watches and interprets, warns and rejoices', and the concomitant ministries of contemplation and re-creation that go with it and undergird it, will be central to this book's understanding of priesthood.

Behind each word is a vast and fascinating scriptural landscape. In what follows, each chapter of this book takes one of these (equally important) words and examines it in greater depth. Whichever of them appeals to us most or seems to suit our temperament best, it is nevertheless when taken together that they build up the paradoxical ambiguity, the challenge and the beauty of priestly ministry.

Let us look at them briefly as a whole, before taking them one at a time.

A priest is called to be a servant *and* shepherd among the people to whom they are sent. In some ways this one sentence perfectly encapsulates the challenge and difficulty of ordained ministry. Some of us may feel temperamentally suited to a ministry that is defined by servanthood. Others may be clear that the call is to leadership. The Ordinal tells us it is both.

To be a servant means, paradoxically, that on the day you become a priest the first thing we tell you is that you never stop being a deacon. But secondly it does assuredly mean that you are a leader, charged with huge and particular responsibility for leading and guiding the people of God, Christ's own flock.

Incidentally, this is also why I get irritated when I hear people being asked the difference between a deacon and a priest and saying 'Oh, there's a few things you can't do as a deacon which you can as a priest', thus writing off their whole vocation in one casual sentence. The 'few things' in question are the declaration of Christ's forgiveness; presidency of the Eucharist; and the announcement of God's blessing. They are hardly incidental! They are the gospel itself: absolution; communion; blessing – things of spiritual value and power that are entrusted to the person who is called and ordained to priestly ministry and who, as such, must receive them with a servant heart. That is why a priest never stops being a deacon, and that priesthood is built upon it. And although it is right that the word 'leader' hardly appears in the New Testament, it is quite plain that in Scripture a shepherd is seen much more as a courageous leader than the gentle pastor we sometimes imagine it might mean today. Although, of course, being a shepherd does also mean caring for the people you serve and making sure they are cared for.

The Christian vocation is not to be a servant *or* a shepherd, but a servant *and* a shepherd, after the example of Christ himself, the Good Shepherd who demonstrates his goodness and his commitment to his flock by laying down his life for them (John 10.11).

Returning to the Ordinal, the next sentence includes the other three deeply fascinating words and build up a beautiful and complex picture of the nature of ordained ministry: a priest is called to be a messenger, sentinel and steward.

To be a messenger is to be someone who is entrusted with the message of the good news of what God has done in Jesus Christ. The effective messenger is the one who is faithful to the message they have received, though its communication in today's world requires huge creativity as we translate the message of the gospel into the smorgasbord of cultures in which we minister. It is therefore a theological as well as an evangelistic task.

To be a sentinel is to be someone who watches and prays, someone who stands on a tower and scans the horizon. It is a lonely and often unpopular vocation. It requires great determination and perseverance. It is a prophetic as well as a contemplative task.

To be a steward is to be someone who is entrusted with responsibility to look after things, to manage, organise and protect them. The priest is steward of the gospel itself and, even more daunting, of the flock of Christ.

The Declaration ends with these sobering words:

> Remember always with thanksgiving that the treasure now to be entrusted to you is Christ's own flock, bought by the shedding of his blood on the cross. It is to him that you will render account for your stewardship of his people.[30]

What sane person, on hearing these words, would not run screaming from the cathedral saying there has been a terrible mistake and they are not fit for this ministry at all? Fortunately, the Declaration continues: 'You cannot bear the weight of this calling in your own strength. Pray therefore that your heart may daily be enlarged.'[31] We will return to the challenge of these words towards the end of the book, but my prayers as you read this is that your heart may be enlarged by considering the priestly vocation through the lens of these words – servant and shepherd, messenger, sentinel and steward.

But before that, two other preliminary matters.

The good ordering of the Church

Throughout this book I am using the language of the Ordinal to describe and understand ordained ministry. Therefore, when I use the word 'ministry' on its own I am primarily thinking about the ministry of the whole people of God, that high and holy calling with which the Ordinal begins every Ordination Service, reminding those who are to be ordained that their first task is to serve this royal priesthood and uphold it in its vocation to share the light of Christ in the world. Then I am calling a deacon a deacon, a priest a priest, and a bishop a bishop. I know that in the Church of England and in other denominations other words are used; but I don't think it is helpful to call the priest 'the minister' since, as will already be apparent, ministry belongs to everyone. As we noted earlier, there is a distinctive Anglican understanding of priesthood, so let's stick with the word.

Neither do I think it appropriate to call the priest 'vicar', since vicar (or for that matter 'rector', 'curate' or 'chaplain') are specific titles that go with specific offices, and it is unhelpful to confuse the two.

When a priest is ordained they are given two pieces of paper. One is called the *Letter of Orders*. It is the formal document that confirms the person's ordination as a deacon or priest in the Church of God. The second piece of paper is the *Licence*. It says that the person is now authorised to exercise their ordained ministry in a particular place and under a particular authority within a particular diocese. The Letter of Orders stays with the deacon and priest throughout their ministry, the proof that they have been ordained; the Licence comes and goes. With each new post there is a new Licence.

Think of the Letter of Orders as being like a driving licence.

It says that the relevant tests have been passed and you are now fit to drive. Unless you do something dreadful, that driving licence stays with you throughout your career as a driver. But you need a vehicle to drive; and with it the relevant vehicle ownership papers. These say that this is your car and you can drive it. But if you change cars, so you will need new papers. This is like the Licence to a particular parish that is given alongside the Letter of Orders. It says as an ordained priest you are able to serve in this place. When the priest moves to a new post a new Licence is issued and the old one relinquished.

The one other term worth mentioning is the one that is put down on legal documents when asked your profession (it is also the term that is used on the Licence itself): Clerk in Holy Orders. This is not a term I would recommend clergy using in their parish, but it is of interest.

The word 'order' and the word 'ordination' share the same root. It is *ordo*, a Latin word used in legal documents and referring to the 'good ordering' of an organisation with appropriate hierarchy and accountability and so on.

The same applies in the Church. To be ordained is to be part of God's good ordering of the Church, with the appropriate leadership and ministry that it needs in order to thrive and fulfil its vocation. A priest is a clerk (also a Latin term *clericus*, from which we get 'cleric' and 'clergy') set apart by ordination to maintain this good order.

This is why on the night before an ordination, and at the Ordination Service itself, the Diocesan Registrar – the lawyer for the diocese – also makes an appearance. He or she leads those about to be ordained in making the necessary oaths and declarations that place their ministry within that wider network of accountability in which everyone must minister.

So by making what is called the Declaration of Assent[32] the new priest gives agreement to the Christian faith as the Church of England has received it. It is important that the ordaining bishop and the people that the new priest will serve know that the person being ordained believes the Christian faith and will proclaim it afresh. They then make an oath of allegiance to the monarch and of canonical obedience to the bishop. These oaths place the new ministry within the larger ministry of the diocese and the national Church. Other denominations have similar practices that make the same point: ministry is not personal property and carries no entitlement of its own. It is held and supported within a wider framework of accountability: the ministry of the whole Church.

During the Ordination Service the Registrar or the Archdeacon is called upon to confirm that these oaths and the Declaration of Assent have been made. And after the Declaration and before the Ordination Prayers the ordinands are asked:

Do you accept the Holy Scriptures as revealing all things necessary for eternal salvation through faith in Jesus Christ?

Will you faithfully minister the doctrine and sacraments of Christ as the Church of England has received them, so that the people committed to your charge may be defended against error and flourish in faith?

Will you accept and minister the discipline of this Church, and respect authority duly exercised within it?[33]

There are other equally important questions about belief and lifestyle, but these three questions in particular give expression to the vital interconnectedness of faith and ministry: that it is something received, which requires good order and that must be passed on to others. Those who are ordained are part of this holy order. The Christian faith is too precious and too important for anyone to think they can go it alone.

Ordained

The warming balm of oil pressed from the olive's virgin crop,
fermenting grapes held for a generation
in the dark womb of their slow gestation,
hands unclenching and reaching out for fresh and fractured bread,
little beads of perspiration on a waiting forehead
as mouth and mind cohere in the unguarded
yes of the terrible decision to turn.

The light dappling the still unconquered waves.
Waiting to break. Everything else behind.
This is where we meet. Every question carried.
Brought to this moment of encounter and
communion. Disturbed. Delivered
into these oh so ordinary hands,
still greasy with the sweat of toil and the stick of Chrism.

STEPHEN COTTRELL

Part Two

CHAPTER TWO

Servant

Be dressed for action and have your lamps lit; be like those who are waiting for their master to return.

LUKE 12.35

In my experience as a bishop, when I speak to those who are at the very early stages of exploring a vocation to ordained ministry and ask them what God might be calling them to, they usually reply that God might be calling them to be a vicar. Or perhaps a priest. Or maybe to ministry or leadership in the Church. But I very rarely hear anyone say that they thought God was calling them to be a deacon. However, everyone who is ordained as a priest in the Church of England, and in many other denominations as well, are ordained a deacon first. Neither does a priest ever stop being a deacon.

There are, therefore, a few things that need to be said about being a deacon which are a vital part of being a priest. First of all, the actual ordination as a deacon usually comes a whole year before the ordination to the priesthood. This can appear a little odd; some people even say that this whole two-step approach to ordination is hopelessly out of date and a silly waste of resources. People are called to the priesthood; they have been trained to be a priest. Why not just get on with it and ordain them as a priest? And if, for the sake of tradition, the Church must insist on being a deacon first, then do it on the quiet during the retreat so that when everyone gets to the cathedral for the ordination service we can get on with the proper stuff. After all, it is confusing enough to church people, let alone to those outside, that having dolled up in our Sunday best for one grand do, we will be invited back again the following year to do it all again! 'Didn't it work the first time?' they will say incredulously.

And another thing: what does a deacon actually do? Deacons go through a very grand ceremony, and at the end of it they have been ordained very publicly to do exactly the same things as they could already do before they started! Virtually all the things that deacons are authorised to do, lay people can do already.

Most deacons won't have taken a funeral before ordination – though those who have been Readers will have done – but that apart, those who are not ordained can preach, teach and serve in all the ways a deacon can. All dressed up, but nowhere to go – that might be a fitting description of a deacon's ministry!

So what exactly is this ordination for? And why doesn't the Church rationalise the process and have done with it?

Well, this is how I see it. The ordination to the diaconate is, first of all, a ministry in its own right. However, it is not measured by tasks fulfilled and responsibilities held, but by its very powerlessness: a deacon is a servant, always pointing beyond themselves, and always putting the needs of others first. This is particularly expressed in the deacon's liturgical role – laying the table, but then stepping aside. Inviting people to share peace with each other. Reading the gospel. Although I hope that before long the Church of England will recover and promote a more thoroughgoing permanent diaconate, similar to other denominations such as the Lutheran churches in Scandinavia, in the Church of England the vast majority of deacons are also called to be priests. Their deaconing, as well as being a ministry in its own right, is also the final preparation and indispensable foundation of all that will follow. Why? Because all ministry is service. Being a deacon is not a stepping stone, but a foundation stone. It is not the apprenticeship year that has to be endured before the real thing – priesthood – starts. It is the foundation upon which everything else is built.

The house built on the rock

Jesus told an interesting story about foundations that is relevant here. It is about two houses. It comes right at the end of the Sermon on the Mount, so for Jesus (and for Matthew) it concludes and sums up the longest teaching passage in the New Testament. Like the opening of Psalm 1, which uses the image of a tree planted in living waters whose leaves do not fade nor fruit fail (Psalm 1.3), Jesus uses the image of a building, stable and strong, and established on firm foundations. In the story one house is built on the rock; the other on the sand. However, if you walked down the street you would not be able to tell the houses apart. They would both appear to be very fine houses. It is only when the crisis comes that one is revealed to be without proper foundations. As the Sunday School song puts it: 'The rains came down and the floods came up and the house on the rock stood firm.'

It is sobering to remember this: the storms will come. There will be times in every ministry when we will be tested.

There will be times when the winds batter. But if our foundations are built upon the rock, we will stand firm.

This does not mean it will not hurt. In the story, both houses are equally battered by the wind and the rain. But only one of them is able to endure. So we must not misunderstand the story. Having good foundations does not mean that we will always have good times. It means we will endure. It means that despite difficulties, hardships and, indeed, the opposition we will face at times, we will flourish.

These foundations, first and foremost, are Christ himself, the one who calls, the one who serves and the one whose gospel saves. But these foundations need to be dug each day. The ordained minister − deacon and priest − will do this through prayer, through brooding upon the Scriptures, through giving proper time each day, each week and each year to rest, retreat, refreshment and replenishing, not just for themselves but for their family and for those they love. We will say more about these things later. However, this might be a good text for anyone contemplating ordained ministry, whatever the denomination, and for all of us who serve the leadership and ministry of the Church: keep the Sabbath day holy (See Exodus 20.8. It is the fifth commandment, one we all tend to break without worry or regret. Perhaps we think we know better than God on this one!).

It will also mean growing in obedience to those to whom we are accountable; it will mean continuing to learn and study the Christian faith and becoming lifelong learners; it will mean asking the Holy Spirit to come upon us each day that we may be changed into the likeness of Christ so that our presence as servants and heralds may be a blessing in the parishes we serve.

Most of all the foundation of the ministry of a deacon is

service. This is what will keep us fixed upon the rock that is Christ, the servant Lord. This in turn will be the foundation of priesthood.

Imagine an anthropologist visiting a cathedral for an ordination of deacons. Imagine that they knew nothing about the Christian tradition, but were well versed in religious phenomena and various initiation rites and practices across the world. Having witnessed the service, if they were then asked what they thought had happened they would say it was obvious. It was some sort of rite of passage in which great authority was being given to those who were now commissioned to leadership within the group. The people receiving the mantle of leadership arrived wearing one set of clothes; they left wearing another. The tribal leader – the one with the pointy hat up the front – had laid hands on each of them in turn and this clearly conveyed the passing on of authority and the sharing in the task of leadership.

But the anthropologist would be wrong. It was, indeed, a rite of passage. Some sort of authority was conveyed. But it was not leadership and, crucially, it was not power. The people at the centre of this rite were not the leaders but the servants. This liturgy was upside down. It was not about the conveyance of authority, but better understood as an embodiment of the Magnificat: the humble are lifted high (see Luke 1.52). The ones at the centre, the ones upon whom great responsibility will be laid, are the lowliest, the servants. The stoles around their necks are best understood as towels of service.

The call to service

Let us, then, return to the Scriptures I quoted at the beginning of this charge: the story from Luke 12 about 'watchful slaves'.

Jesus says this:

> Be dressed for action and have your lamps lit; be like those
> who are waiting for their master to return from the wedding
> banquet, so that they may open the door for him as soon as
> he comes and knocks.
>
> LUKE 12.35-6

The context for this in Luke's Gospel is Jesus teaching his
disciples about a simplicity of life, seeking the unfailing treas-
ures of heaven (Luke 12.33) and knowing it is the Father's
good pleasure to give them the kingdom (Luke 12.32). It is
fairly familiar ground: those who follow Jesus must be servants; they must be ready for action, their lamps lit, etc. So
it goes on: 'Blessed are those slaves whom the master finds
alert when he comes' (Luke 12.37a). So far so good, but if
we're honest, rather predictable. The servants are ready. They
are waiting for their master. When he does return – whatever
the hour – they are there to wait upon him and to serve his
every need. This is surely where the story is leading.

Then there is a shocking and dramatic twist. Unexpectedly
– so unexpectedly, I sometimes wonder whether this is another
of those passages from Scripture that we read, but never
inwardly digest – Jesus says this: 'Truly I tell you, he [the
Master] will fasten his belt and have them sit down to eat,
and he will come and serve them' (Luke 12.37b). The long-
awaited master does not sit down and expect the servants to
wait on him. He does not call for food and drink for himself.
He does not bark out his orders, though as the master he
would be entitled to do so. Rather, he invites them, the servants, to sit down. *He waits on them.*

This is a remarkable reversal of expectations. In fact, it

is the last thing we expect. But it illustrates perfectly the character and purposes of the God we serve, and of Jesus' own identity as the one 'who comes not to be served, but to serve' (Matthew 20.28).

In other words, whenever Jesus speaks about the life of discipleship, about ministry, about the apostolic life, he always speaks about servanthood first, and in his own life embodies this servant ministry.

The Ordinal reflects this priority of service. In the Introduction to the liturgy we read:

Deacons are ordained so that the people of God may be better equipped to make Christ known. Theirs is a life of visible self-giving. Christ is the pattern of their calling and their commission; as he washed the feet of his disciples, so they must wash the feet of others.[1]

In fact this reference to Jesus washing his disciples' feet is mentioned twice in the Ordination Service for deacons: here at the very beginning, and again in the Ordination Prayer itself. And, as if to emphasise the point and drill it home, when a deacon does get to be ordained to the priesthood, the Declaration begins by saying that 'Priests are called to be servants...'[2] Which is another way of saying a priest is called to be a deacon! In other words, you never stop being a deacon. You never stop being called to wash feet. You never put the towel down. The diaconate is the heart and the heartbeat of all ministry. Christ is one who serves – the one who serves us, who are his servants – and we best follow him and emulate him by serving others ourselves.

And a deacon is a herald of the gospel (a messenger), a servant of Christ who serves Christ's people. It is the deacon's powerlessness, the very lack of authority to do the things that are most associated with ordained ministry, that gives the deacon the power of love, self-giving and self-effacing. In this way, a deacon always points beyond themselves, is always upending people's expectations; is always exercising their ministry in the networks of the world.

This point is emphasised in the Ordinal. Although it makes it clear that the work of the deacon cannot be separated from the work of the bishop and the priests with whom they serve – and right at the beginning of the service in the Introduction it says that they are ordained 'so that the people of God may be better equipped to make Christ known'[3] – the specific and distinctive marks of the deacon's ministry are as 'agents of God's purposes of love', serving the community in which they are set, and 'bringing to the Church the needs and hopes of all the people', especially 'searching out the poor and weak, the sick and the lonely, and those who are oppressed and powerless'; and then – in a most striking phrase – it adds that deacons must 'reach into the forgotten corners of the world, so the love of God may be made visible'.[4]

Then it says, almost by the way, that deacons will also do the odd thing in church – helping lead the worship and preaching from time to time.

There is also a beautiful symmetry of the call to 'bring to the Church the needs and hopes of all the people' and to 'bring the needs of the world before the Church in prayer'. The service runs in two directions; outward in service to the world, but then back to the Church offering the greatest service of all, which is the communion with God that we enjoy in prayer and worship and into which we bring the needs and hopes of all the people we serve.

Another way of expressing this is to say that the deacon

is always looking for the Master's return, and searches him out, especially among the poor, the oppressed and those who are powerless themselves. We long to greet him and receive him. A deacon has nothing to offer except this burning desire to serve Christ.

So I exhort deacons never to fall into the trap of apologising over the funny ways we do things in the Church of England. There is ancient wisdom here. A deacon will best be made ready to receive the authority that comes with priestly ministry, by enduring and enjoying this strange, neither fish nor fowl, year of deaconing, where you look to all the world (and all the Church!) like any other ordained minister, but are not. And because priesthood does involve receiving spiritual authority to absolve in the name of Christ, to preside at the Eucharist, to announce God's blessing – then this must be received with a humble, servant heart: the heart of a deacon. And because the heart is a muscle and, like all muscles, grows by being exercised, the Ordinal also exhorts deacons to read the Scriptures, building foundations of rest and prayer, and be watchful for the presence of God in the world. These are the exercises of the heart, and we will say much more about them later in the book. But they are also foundations that need to be established from the beginning.

The ministry of a deacon is not easy. It will often be misunderstood. Much of what a deacon does will be away from the spotlight of presiding at worship or taking centre stage at meetings and gatherings. It won't seem economic or productive or useful; and the deacon might sometimes feel unappreciated and underused. And occasionally this ministry will be rejected. Remember how Peter argued with Jesus, saying that it shouldn't be Jesus washing his feet, but the other way around. To be served is sometimes just as hard as serving. Many will recoil from it. And we too, the servants of Christ, will need to learn how to receive from others, lest we end up making our own service a form of power. But here is the point: by paying attention to the exercises of the heart and by living as one who serves others, and is at the same time open and vulnerable to others, and who is a voice and herald of the gospel (which is itself God's service to the world), the deacon becomes a visible, tangible and practical presence of God for others.

Therefore, the year of serving as a deacon, a year of pointing beyond yourself to others and to God, will be the best preparation for a ministry that can never be anything other than the ministry of Christ through the power of the Spirit. It is my hope, then, that deacons will enjoy being deacons, and not spend the year wishing it were over and the 'real ministry' could begin. In fact, it may be the very best opportunity to release and encourage ministry in others. Because this year, more than any other, will not be about anything a deacon does themselves, but always about who they are and where they point.

Moreover, this servant-heartedness will shape the strategy of our ministry as servant leaders. I heard recently of a church in East London, where I serve, that had developed three principles about mission that embody this servant-hearted leadership. They proposed that whenever they had an idea to do something in and for their community, they first thought, 'Who is already doing this?', or something like it; let us ask if we could join them. Then, secondly, if they couldn't think of anyone, they would ask 'Who might be interested in doing something like this?' and see if they would like to join forces with us. Only if the answer was 'no' to these two questions would they ever undertake an initiative on their own.

This is servant leadership, serving the community and looking to build coalitions of goodwill, where there is mutual giving and receiving. It is a way of leading that is shaped by diaconal hearts.

A ministry of surprises

Finally, a deacon should be ready for a surprise.

Most people, when they get to the Ordination Service itself, have a rough idea of why they are being ordained and why God has called them into ministry. But let me give you this assurance: they are probably wrong. God has got all sorts of ideas up his copious sleeve, and ordination is a sacrament, a real and effective sign of God's goodness and grace; and by the grace of holy orders – that is, not just a passing out ceremony in which we congratulate the newly ordained on their academic successes and their all-round goodness and suitability, but a fresh anointing of the Spirit for the purposes of God that are bigger and wilder and more profligate than we could possibly imagine.

Look what happened to the first deacons! The reason they were set apart for service could hardly have been clearer. In Acts 6, Luke puts it plainly:

> The twelve called together the whole community of the disciples and said, 'It is not right that we should neglect the word of God in order to wait at tables. Therefore, friends, select from among yourselves seven men of good standing, full of the Spirit and of wisdom, whom we may appoint to this task, while we, for our part, will devote ourselves to prayer and to serving the word.'

> ACTS 6.2–4

The instructions are very straightforward. Or as we would put it in today's Church of England, the statement of particulars, the role description and the working agreement have all been properly agreed: wait at tables, keep the accounts, and look after the widows. But just a few verses later on, we find Stephen doing signs and wonders among the people, preaching before the Sanhedrin, and then being martyred for his efforts. And in Acts 8 Philip is preaching and church planting in Samaria.

This is good news: the gospel is spreading fast, and people are being saved; but 'Who is waiting at the tables?' is not an unreasonable question to ask. It is certainly not those who were set apart for the task. The Holy Spirit has already led them on to something else.

So let us be wary of ever thinking we've got ordination or ministry too worked out. Let us be wary of those who tell us about patterns of ministry in the New Testament. My only conclusion is this: the Holy Spirit is Lord of the Church, and it is God we must serve and God we must wait upon. And so, to those who are ordained or to those just thinking about ordination I say this: be people of prayer, wait patiently upon God and, like watchful servants, be dressed for action and have your lamps lit; open the door for the Lord when he comes and look out for him, for his coming will nearly always be a surprise. Allow the Spirit to lead you; and test your conclusions and your intuitions against the mind of the Church. Be obedient to the gospel and to those in authority, for you are a servant, and at the end of the day all that is expected is your faithfulness.

CHAPTER THREE

Shepherd

Keep watch over yourselves and over the flock, of which the
Holy Spirit has made you overseers, to shepherd the
Church of God that he has obtained with the blood of his
own Son.

ACTS 20.28

Describing a priest as a shepherd has a marvellous biblical
pedigree. Jeremiah and Ezekiel and many others refer to those
who lead the people of God as shepherds.[1] Jesus is himself
the Good Shepherd, and here in Acts 20, those whom the
Holy Spirt has called to a ministry of oversight (bishop) and
those who by extension share this ministry as priests, are also
called shepherds. But it is also problematic. Most of us today
know very little about shepherds and shepherding. It is not
part of our everyday experience. If we know about it at all
it is from books or television, and usually, in an English
context, involves a sheepdog doing most of the work while
the shepherd whistles instructions from the sidelines.

Perhaps this is why we feel unsure about calling ourselves
shepherds, and at the same time have turned the word
'pastoral', and with it 'pastoral ministry' into something
rather insipid, as if to be pastoral was just about keeping

people happy and being nice to them. Conversely, it might also be why some clergy are uncomfortable with the language of leadership. We haven't realised what a shepherd's job actually involves.

When the shepherd boy David is questioned over his credentials and ability to face the monster Goliath, he retorts by saying, 'Whenever a lion or a bear came, and took a lamb from the flock, I went after it and struck it down, rescuing the lamb from its mouth; and if it turned against me, I would catch it by the jaw, and kill it' (1 Samuel 17.34–5). I don't know how much time is spent learning how to grab bears by the jaw or kill lions in today's pastoral theology lectures, but here is the raw and unadorned description of pastoral leadership: to lay down one's life for the sheep (see John 10.15).

Indeed this is how shepherds operated in New Testament times. They would live alongside their sheep. Sometimes their own body was the gate to the fold, lying down in the entrance to keep predators at bay. When they directed the flock to new pastures, they led from the front, striding out ahead of the sheep; and when a lion or a bear did threaten the flock, the shepherd was ready and equipped to fight them off. It is with this in mind that Pope Francis has famously spoken of his wish for priests 'with the smell of the sheep', that is priests who so live alongside and with the people they serve that they even smell like them.[2]

This is also what Jesus means when he says he is a Good Shepherd. He was the one who so loved the sheep that he was prepared to lay down his life for them (John 10.11). Note how in this passage Jesus also contrasts the true shepherd, who knows his sheep and whose sheep know him, with the hired hand whose lack of concern for the sheep is illustrated by the fact that even though he sees the wolf approaching, he flees, saving his own skin and abandoning the flock. This too is the reason why when Peter, having failed Jesus so blatantly, swears that he loves him, is given the instruction: 'Feed my sheep, tend for my lambs' (See John 21.15–17). This is the work of those who love Christ: to care for the flock for whom Christ died; to be committed to them and not to abandon them; to love them and to know them.

However, there is also a danger here. If by 'knowing the sheep', we mean 'knowing each of them personally', then we may as well put a 'full up' sign outside the church once our congregation has grown to a certain size.

Have you noticed how some congregations – usually in suburban areas – never get much bigger than about a hundred to a hundred and fifty people? This is not necessarily because they have become complacent or stopped doing evangelism. It is far more likely to be a pastoral care issue. The priest probably sees themselves as a pastor and a shepherd. A male priest may even enjoy being called 'Father'; and what father does not know each of his children by name? As Jesus says, 'the good shepherd knows the sheep' (see John 10.14). But any one person can only 'know' so many others. If our model of leadership and ministry is based around our ability to have a meaningful relationship with each member of the congregation we will probably have a happy church, but its size will be limited, its people dependent, and its priest exhausted.

I was that priest once. I was privileged and excited to be the leader of a rapidly growing church, whose congregation doubled in about three years. When the numbers coming on Sunday reached about a hundred and fifty people and it was a real challenge to manage the growth and the diversity of the operation, I thought the answer was that I just needed to work harder and run faster. But there weren't any more hours in the day. At the same time, I was feeling guilty: I didn't know everybody in the congregation like I used to.

The answer that I slowly discovered is one I have already mentioned, but is vital if we are to understand properly the relationship between ordained ministry and the ministry of the whole people of God. It is important that people are known. 'Being known' and 'feeling you belong' is vital for church growth and for church health. But it didn't have to be my job to do all the 'knowing'. Rather, I had to become the one who created the structures and nurtured the wider network of relationships, and with this the other ministries and leadership needed to make it happen, so that people would feel known and have a sense of belonging. But it wouldn't all be down to my personal effort or ability. I would be the one who would be responsible for the whole ministry of the church, not the person who had to do the whole ministry myself. I had to stop being the chaplain to the congregation – a trap too many clergy fall into: they call it pastoral, but it is really simply keeping people happy – or, for that matter, just the evangelist out in the community. I had to be the shepherd: the leader who took responsibility for the well-being of the flock. By understanding my role as shepherd, I could become the leader in mission (real pastoral ministry) and the church could grow again and have a greater impact in more people's lives and in the community we were called to serve.

It was probably the most important and the most painful lesson I have learned in over thirty years of ordained ministry. It was the biggest single failing of my preparation for ordained ministry: that despite all the very good things I learned, nothing had prepared me for these very specific responsibilities of pastoral leadership; to be the one who led the church, and that as leader in mission I would – God willing! –enable that church to grow as much by its exercise of pastoral care as its evangelism and service, alongside the quality of its worship. Sharing ministry and developing structures of pastoral care so that everyone was known and everyone belonged became the key to sustaining a growth that was going to burn itself out (along with me!) if I persisted with a model of leadership that was dependent upon my own ability to know everyone.

I hope things are different nowadays. Sometimes I doubt it. We are still turning out clergy who think ministry is their job alone; or who feel leadership is either beneath them or beyond them. But the introduction to the ordination liturgy for priests puts it succinctly: 'Priests are to set the example of the Good Shepherd always before them as the pattern of their calling.'[3] It is what we see in Christ's ministry and leadership that is the pattern for ours.

Available to God

To be a shepherd is to be a leader in the Church, but it is also to be a leader who is constantly investing in others. Just for a moment, pause to consider the disproportionate amount of time Jesus gave to a few people, how incredibly *unavailable* he was so much of the time, disappearing to pray and finding joy with all sorts of unlikely people and in all sorts of unexpected places; how he was so good at saying 'no' as well as saying 'yes', turning his back on needs in one place in order to preach the gospel in another (see, for instance, Mark 1.37–9).

This, too, should be the pattern of all priestly ministry, because it is the ministry of Christ, it is his flock we care for, and unless we are rooted in him, we will not be able to do anything (see John 15.5).

Preaching about Christ as the One True Shepherd, St Augustine said: 'All good shepherds are in the one shepherd; they are one. They feed the sheep, and Christ feeds them.'[4] This one beautiful sentence makes it clear that the ordained minister is a shepherd to the flock of Christ, and yet is dependent upon Christ who is the one, true shepherd. The one who leads is also the one who serves, and can only feed others – for the job of the shepherd is the well-being, safety and flourishing of the sheep – if they are being fed by Christ themselves. In another sermon Augustine says, 'I feed you on what I am fed myself. I am just a servant.'[5]

This is why the first two words in the Declaration in the Ordinal must be read together: a servant *and* a shepherd, not a servant *or* a shepherd. Servant leadership, leadership like Christ, the one who serves and leads, is the hallmark of every Christian priest.

Finally, this is also a ministry where the people of God – those we lead and serve – have a right to expect from us a certain expertise and ability. This is hard to talk about. We have so downplayed this aspect of vocation that there is a danger it appears to be only about a personal call from God (and the role of the Church just to rubber stamp that which God has already foretold in the life of the would-be priest!). But in previous times there was far greater emphasis on the call of the Church. I think this is very important, for when we say being a priest is 'more than job' (which it is), this doesn't mean it is 'less than a job'. It means it is everything we would expect from a job – i.e. a set of competencies and abilities that we can reasonably measure, plus more. So, for instance, if one visited a doctor, complaining about some knee ache or whatever, and the doctor sat back in his chair and said that unfortunately he had been absent during the lectures on knees and could offer no advice, you might conclude that this person is not a doctor in any even-handed estimation of what it is reasonable to expect a doctor to be. It is not that you expect them to be an expert in knee aches (after an initial diagnosis it may turn out that you need to be referred to a consultant) but that you rightly expect them to know *something*, and to be able to offer some assistance.

So it is with priests. The people we lead and serve should reasonably expect us to be proficient and, to a certain degree, 'expert' in certain things: firstly, in the things of God, the life of prayer and the spiritual pathways we must follow, with all their attendant dangers, darkness and snares; also in the study and knowledge of God, chiefly, the Scriptures them-selves, but also liturgy and doctrine; and then in pastoral skills, by which I mean the actual leading of the church. St Ambrose puts this sharply: 'Who is going to entrust himself to someone whose wisdom seems to be no greater than his own? Who wants to quench his thirst with dirty water?'[6]

But neither do we lead simply because we have a certain knowledge or expertise, still less the institutional authority that comes with ordination. We lead because we have been called, and because we are striving to live a virtuous Christ-like life, that is itself the verification of our ministry. This is what Paul means when he says that we do not need letters of recommendation. Our lives are a letter from Christ, written by the Holy Spirit on our hearts (see 2 Corinthians 3.1–3).

No one approaching ordination will have all the skills that are needed, nor will anyone ever need all of them (though every priest must be knowledgeable about prayer and belief), but the virtues that mean we lead out of our own dependence on the Spirit of God are vital for every priest. In the Church of England a period of formation and training at a residential theological college or a regional course will be followed by a curacy where the new deacon is placed with an experienced incumbent in a parish or in a group of parishes. This curacy is still part of the training. There is a weaving together of practical, theoretical and formational development. At the end of it there will be some proper evaluation of how someone has grown in ordained ministry so that the Church can be confident that those who are called to the very specific leadership responsibilities that go with the incumbency of a parish are ready for this big step.

Different ways of exercising priestly ministry

It is no longer sufficient (perhaps it never has been) to think of every priest in the same way. Although many clergy will exercise most of their ministry as incumbents of parishes – as vicars – I am increasingly aware that priesthood is actually exercised in many different ways. There is a basic set of competencies, attributes and attitudes that every priest requires. As I have already indicated, these are primarily based around our need for every priest to be able to lead people in the ways of God, through prayer and the study and communication of the faith itself, and by the centrality of their own lifelong discipleship. This is the core vocation shared by every priest and summed up in the notion that the priest is first of all a minister of word and sacrament.

For some clergy it will never be more than this. They will exercise their priesthood in ways that are 'diaconal', serving the spiritual and theological needs of the Church. Their leadership will be in a supportive role. Others will have what is called 'the cure of souls', that is the care for every person who lives in that parish and community. They will be those who go on to take a much greater responsibility for leadership and whose priesthood will be more obviously 'episcopal' in the ways we have already discussed. This is rooted in the New Testament pattern where, for instance in 1 Peter 5, the elders of the Church (the Greek word used is *presbyteroi*) are exhorted 'to tend the flock of God that is in your charge, exercising the oversight (*episkopountes*), not under compulsion but willingly, as God would have you do it' (1 Peter 5.3). Such melding together of the words 'presbyter/priest' and 'episcopacy/bishop' shows both how the threefold pattern for ministry we have inherited started to emerge, and also how in the early Church these roles, and the leadership responsibilities that went with them, developed.

Then there are all sorts of other ways that some priests exercise their priestly ministry – in chaplaincies in schools, colleges of further education, universities, prisons and hospitals; as pioneer ministers planting new churches; as theological educators or as members of religious orders. All involve a servant leadership after the pattern of Christ the Good Shepherd, the one who came to serve, but all have different emphases between the 'serving' and the 'leading'.

Neither has any of this got anything to do with whether a priest will receive a stipend or not. Some of the greatest leadership will be exercised by self-supporting priests in their work place as well as in the oversight of the Church (as, for instance, an area dean). Moreover, the most diaconal ministry is often exercised by those in paid chaplaincy positions, serving right outside the institutional life of the Church and among those most on the edge and in deepest need.

We should, therefore, leave behind the questions about whether ministry is full-time or part-time. It is always both.

All of us are full-time priests. Our ordination confers upon us a responsibility and an identity that cannot be put on and taken off, as if it were merely a job. All of us are part-time. We are properly limited by the time we can offer to ministry by the equally important responsibilities of family or of other paid employment. Let us, therefore, stop using this unhelpful language. We are all priests, serving the Church in different ways according to our different circumstances, and according to the different ways the Church has called and equipped us. We will return to this important subject.

In its selection and training of those to be ordained, the Church has not always been good at noticing all these differences.[7] Perhaps when we were ministering in a more settled environment, where the Christian faith was better known and the Church better attended, such a differentiation between different ways of exercising priesthood was not so important. In the missionary situation we face today it is. We need greater wisdom in discerning what is common to the call of every priest, and what are the very different ways priesthood is expressed in what goes with and is rightly expected from the particular licence and ministry of a particular calling and particular missionary or pastoral need. One size does not fit all in a missionary Church. Peter's call and vocation was different from Paul's. Ours will be too.

Absolution and blessing

When it comes to that funny business of explaining to friends and family – even those who go to Church – why you get ordained twice, deacons, as I noted earlier, are sometimes tempted to say that there are one or two things you can't do as a deacon that you can as a priest: declare absolution;

preside at Holy Communion; and bless in the name of the Lord. Not incidental things by any means! We will say more about presiding at Communion later on, but let me finish this chapter thinking about absolution and blessing, for these are certainly the works of a good shepherd.

On the first night of Easter Jesus gave authority to his disciples to continue his ministry in the world. He breathed on them and said, 'Receive the Holy Spirit. If you forgive the sins of any, they are forgiven them'(John 20.22–3). This authority is sometimes referred to as the power of the keys. The keys of heaven, the keys of forgiveness, are entrusted to us. It is not that we have any power to open the gates of heaven, or any power to forgive sins, but we are given the authority to speak and act in the name of Jesus himself, who does.

The most obvious sign of this in the week-in-week-out life of a priest is that we say the Prayer of Absolution in the liturgy. But it is more than this: the gospel itself is the good news of reconciliation with God. Either that or it has simply become good advice.

Furthermore, it is reconciliation with each other. As it states in the letter to the Ephesians, Christ is our peace:

in his flesh he has made both groups [that is, Jews and Gentiles, in other words everyone] into one and has broken down the dividing wall, that is, the hostility between us. He has abolished the law with its commandments and ordinances, that he might create in himself one new humanity in place of the two, thus making peace, and might reconcile both groups to God in one body through the cross

EPHESIANS 2.14–16

The priest is the one who is declaring this reconciliation and therefore the minister and sign of these new relationships we have with God and with each other.

In today's world there is a further dimension to this that we urgently need to rediscover: reconciliation with the earth itself. For too long we have seen ourselves as having dominion over the earth. We therefore used and abused the earth in whatever ways suited us. We forgot that we were part of this creation and called to be its stewards. We simply saw it as a resource that we could plunder at will, and we were blind to the terrible consequences of our actions, first among the poorest of the world, and then – the situation we now face – imperilling the life of the earth itself. We used to say the damage being done was unimaginable. But now we don't need to imagine it; we can see the consequences of our misuse all around us in flood and famine, in forest fires and poisoned air. We need to rediscover that ancient vocation to be good stewards of the earth, and this vocation flows from those other biblical images of tending and caring, such as being also a good shepherd.

We need to amend our lives and learn to live peaceably on the earth, honouring and safeguarding its equilibrium. And the Church must take a lead in calling the whole world to think again and change its ways.

Jesus' ministry begins with the word 'repent' (see Mark 1.15). It is not a fashionable word. Our culture is not comfortable with the notion of sin. However, when we look at what we are doing to the world, when we consider the divisions that are between us in our world at the moment, when we give even half a thought to the ways in which we hurt and exploit each other, then even if we don't choose to use the word 'sin', we do acknowledge that the world is not as it is meant to be, and our own lives are not as they should be.

Nevertheless, I was surprised and encouraged when I found myself being interviewed by, of all people, the comedian, writer and activist Russell Brand. I was the guest on his weekly *Under the Skin* podcast. He quizzed me about the Christian faith and at one point I found myself needing to say something a bit more challenging about the demands of Christian discipleship (I was fearing the whole thing was sounding a bit too cosy). I said to him that the first word Jesus uttered in his ministry was 'repent' and I explained it meant turn around; you're going in the wrong direction. I was relating this to the context of our own lives and to the life of our whole world. I thought he might balk at the idea; that it might appear to be asking too much. But on the contrary he was hugely excited by the concept. This is what he said:

> This turning around, that would mean, my instinctive reaction to that concept is turn around from pleasure and face purpose, turn around from a material life and face a spiritual life; turn around from self-service and embrace service of others.[8]

It's not a bad description of the Christian life and the challenge of repentance. And he was excited by the challenge. However, my fear for our proclamation of the gospel today is not that we frighten people away by the challenge of the gospel, but that we do not set the bar high enough. We ask too little. And this is particularly what I hear from young people, who don't want to just go to Church, but might be intrigued and compelled by a turned-around life. They are the ones who seem to care most about what is happening to the planet, for instance. They are calling out for new direction.

What the Christian faith offers is a whole new way of inhabiting the world and a whole new way of relating to God and a whole new way of being human. This is very compelling. And very challenging. We enter it not through our hard work or our imagined goodness, but by turning and embracing what God offers us in Christ. In Christ God shows us how we might live differently. This affects and changes all our relationships: our relationship with God; our relationship with ourselves; our relationships with each other; our relationship with the earth. Therefore to be the one who declares absolution is to be the one who declares the gospel of reconciliation; who calls upon people to turn around and live differently: to embrace purpose. This must be the content of all our preaching and teaching. We must not lose any opportunity to lay before people the beauty and the challenge of the gospel.

Mostly this will be done through the ordinary everyday networks of parish and pioneer ministry. But there is also a specific call upon us. There will be people in the parishes and communities where we serve who are carrying great burdens of personal sin and who long to receive the affirmation of God's love, God's acceptance, and God's forgiveness. It is the greatest medicine. For some people, the way to do this will be through the specific channel of grace that we call the sacrament of reconciliation. Priests need particular training for this. Contrary to the belief that it's just some high church practice that is only relevant for some, to make a confession of sin in the presence of a priest is simply to do in one very open, vulnerable and transparent way what every Christian should be trying to do every day, which is to bring our lives, and especially those things that are still hidden in darkness, into the light of Christ.

Therefore as well as the huge global issues where hubris, vanity and neglect corrupt our world, in the day-to-day pastoral ministry of any church, and especially at services of renewal where prayer ministry is offered, the priest will often encounter the longing of the human heart for a better way, to turn from the reality of sin, and the desire to be forgiven.

A couple of years ago I ordained one of our locally deployed self-supporting priests. Let's call him David. He had had very little formal education. He was, I think, in his early sixties. He trained on our one-year pathway. He wasn't ever going to be in charge of a parish. He was ordained to serve in the small village community where he had lived all his life. At the interview I had with him before his priesting, he expressed concern that he didn't feel trained or equipped to hear people's confessions. I told him not to worry. First, there would be some training as part of the training programme in his curacy, and secondly, newly ordained priests shouldn't really hear confessions until they had received the training. Moreover, in rural parishes like his he was unlikely to encounter queues of people wanting to make their confession!

That was a few years ago. Earlier this year I visited David's parish. It was actually my second visit in less than a year. The reason I've been twice is that there are many people getting confirmed in this little rural community. After the service we were having a cup of tea and David reminded me of that conversation. 'Bishop,' he said, 'you were wrong.' 'What do you mean?' I enquired. He said that hearing confessions was one of the main things he was doing and one of the main drivers for growth and renewal in the parish.

I also remember a conversation with a professor of child and adolescent psychiatry who was not particularly a person of faith. He worked with some of the most broken and damaged young people you can imagine, those living with debilitating mental illnesses, but also survivors of terrible abuse; and those who had done some dark and terrible things themselves. He said to me that there was one thing that he knew many of his patients needed that he didn't have the means or authority to provide. 'What's that?' I asked him. 'Forgiveness,' he replied. 'That is what so many of the people I serve need. They can't forgive themselves. They don't know who else can. They long to know that they can be loved, accepted and forgiven. We can offer the first two, but not the third.'

Finally a priest is called to bless. This is probably the aspect of priestly ministry that is spoken about the least, and yet as I get older – and perhaps especially because I am a bishop and this is the one thing I always do – I increasingly think of it as the most important and the most beautiful, because to bless things in the name of the Lord requires generosity and discernment. We need to decide what to bless and, I suppose, what not to bless. And when we bless we are asking that God's goodness and God's abundance rests upon and flows into that person or even that thing, because, as well as people, we might be called upon to bless all sorts of other objects or endeavours as well. I remember in my very first week of being a priest a woman in the street asking me to bless her buggy. I was happy to do it. I prayed for God's goodness and protection to surround the buggy and the children it carried.

In Marilynne Robinson's book, *Gilead,* the hero, Revd John Ames, remarks:

'I became a minister not for any of the usual reasons, but because it gave me the opportunity to confer blessing.' He says that's one of the advantages of being a minister, not that you have to be a minister to confer blessing; you are simply much more likely to find yourself in that position. 'It's a thing people expect of you.'[9]

I heard my colleague, Bishop Roger Morris, preaching about this one Maundy Thursday: 'What a beautiful way of understanding our role', he reflected. 'We exist in order to confer blessing.'[10]

Binding this together with what I have already said about forgiveness as well as blessing, John Ames reminds us of this important truth: 'to be forgiven is only half the gift. The other half is that *we* also can forgive, restore, and liberate, and therefore we can feel the will of God enacted through us, which is the great restoration of ourselves to ourselves.'[11] As we pray in the Lord's Prayer each day, as well as asking forgiveness for ourselves, *we forgive the sins of others*. And bearing in mind what I said above about reconciliation with the earth, what a difference it might make to the world if we could pray that other line from the Lord's Prayer, asking only for the bread we need today and not always expecting more.

The advice in the first letter of Peter is that we should have a 'unity of spirit, sympathy, love for one another, a tender heart, and a humble mind'. He goes on: 'Do not repay evil for evil or abuse for abuse; but, on the contrary, repay with a blessing'(1 Peter 3.8–9). By living this sort of life we become ourselves, truly as we are meant to be in Christ.

This is the vocation that God is calling people to. God is calling people from the very first moment of their being. It may take a long while for people to respond, or even to realise God is calling, though some may have known it as a small child but never spoken about it until years later. It may come in a single gulp of grace (as St Cyprian a third-century bishop of the Church described it) or at the end of a long and arduous struggle. But this is the calling of ordained ministry. God wishes to enact his will through the ordinary men and women God calls. They become the means whereby God forgives, restores, heals, feeds and blesses his people so that they too may be his transforming presence in the world, also blessing and providing. The priest as shepherd caring for and protecting the flock shows people what Christian love and Christian service looks like.

In doing this, each priest becomes more the person they were meant to be. This has always been my experience of the priesthood. Who I am has not been lost, compromised or diminished by my priesthood, though, of course, there have been times when it is hard and challenging and lonely, and many times where I have felt ill-equipped and unworthy to face the demands of ministry; but through it all I feel that ordination has made me more the person I am meant to be. It has expanded me. God seems to have completed something in me, or perhaps I should say 'is in the process of completing me' through the outpouring and anointing of his Spirit in the grace of holy orders.

I am restored to myself. And in knowing and accepting my need of God and allowing God's Holy Spirit to do her stuff in me, then I am able to be open and vulnerable to others, more able to forgive and to bless – even those who hurt me – and, then, for Christ to be so alive in me that I am completely myself, even an icon of Christ.

CHAPTER FOUR

Messenger

In the presence of God and of Christ Jesus, who is to
judge the living and the dead, and in view of his appearing
and his kingdom, I solemnly urge you: proclaim the
message; be persistent whether the time is favourable or
unfavourable; convince, rebuke, and encourage, with the
utmost patience in teaching. For the time is coming when
people will not put up with sound doctrine, but having
itching ears, they will accumulate for themselves teachers
to suit their own desires, and will turn away from listening
to the truth and wander away to myths. As for you, always
be sober, endure suffering, do the work of an evangelist,
carry out your ministry fully.

2 TIMOTHY 4.1–5

In the declaration that is made at every ordination service,
the work of a priest is described in this way:

With their Bishop and fellow ministers, they are to proclaim
the word of the Lord and to watch for the signs of God's
new creation. They are to be messengers, sentinels and stewards of the Lord; they are to teach and admonish, to feed
and provide for his family, to search for his children in the

wilderness of this world's temptations, and to guide them through its confusions, that they may be saved through Christ for ever. Formed by the word, they are to call their hearers to repentance and to declare in Christ's name the absolution and forgiveness of their sins. With all God's people they are to tell the story of God's love.[1]

The person who is called to be servant and shepherd is now also called to be messenger, sentinel and steward. In this chapter we are going to look clearly and boldly at the vocation to be a messenger.

At first sight it is blindingly simple and obvious. The job of a messenger is to deliver a message! You have not written the message. You have just received it. There may be things about it you don't understand. There may even be bits you disagree with or think should be amended in some way. But it is not your job to alter or embroider it. You just need to pass it on. What could be more straightforward?

Well, quite a lot, actually. The message that we proclaim is both startlingly simple and, at the same time, inexhaustibly rich and complex: for the message that we are called to bear to the world is the Word of God, that Word which is from the beginning, and through whom the whole world has its being, the Word that was made flesh in Jesus Christ (see John 1.1–14).

The message of the Christian faith can never be reduced to a formula or a slogan. Neither can it ever be completely contained within a creed, though we do importantly have the creedal boundary commissions of our faith to work within. Neither should it be constrained or reduced by the limitations of human imagination or intellect, though this often happens. For us Christians, the message and the messenger are one. The message we bear is Jesus himself.

If you did force me to describe it in a nutshell, I would suggest something like: The message of the Christian faith is the invitation to enjoy the fullness of life with God. This is the phrase Jesus uses in John's Gospel. He declares that he has come to bring us life in all its fullness (See John 10.10). This fullness of life has been secured for us through the death and resurrection of Jesus Christ; through him we have peace with God and access to God. That is why the New Testament so often describes the gospel as one of reconciliation. It is also why, as we explored in the last chapter, one of the over-whelming privileges of priestly ministry is to declare absolution, and sometimes in the sobering intimacy of the sacrament of reconciliation to offer God's forgiveness one to one. Such offering of forgiveness and speaking about recon-ciliation is one of the ways the message of the Christian faith is communicated. But it is never just a message for someone else. All of us need to receive the invitation of forgiveness we declare to others and make it our own. As Gregory the Great observed, 'The hand that would cleanse others must itself be cleansed, or it will soil everything that it touches.'[2]

God in Jesus Christ has already done everything that is necessary for us to enjoy fullness of life with him. This is simply a message to be announced (the gospel is, after all, good news not good advice!). It does need appropriating, however, for it only makes sense when it is lived and entered into. The Word was made flesh; God sent a man – Jesus Christ. The ministers of this gospel must not turn it back into a word. And they must not turn it into a manifesto. In scripture God gives us a story not a statement.

This is what the Ordinal states: 'Tell the story of God's love.' Priests and all ministers of the gospel need to tell the story winningly and creatively and let its truth emerge. They need to deliver the invitation and then stay around to talk afterwards, because the gospel will always challenge, irritate, intrigue, delight and provoke. But it is not the job of the minister to convert people. They will always fail. Conversion is the work of the Holy Spirit. Rather, the vocation is to be a storyteller, a witness to God's story in their own lives; to be a messenger, delivering the invitation that comes direct from the cross of Christ; to be a living signpost whose own life directs others to the way of Christ. And to trust that the God who converted them will convert others.

'You yourselves are God's letter of recommendation' writes Paul to the church in Corinth (See 2 Corinthians 3.1–3). Priests, therefore, need to embody and demonstrate the words they proclaim. They need to let the Holy Spirit write them on their hearts, for if we believe that God has made a new humanity in Jesus Christ, then we must live it out each day. The priest's life of gentleness, forbearance, humility, and a readiness to forgive others because they know how much they need to be forgiven themselves, will speak of the gospel.

At the same time, and especially in a culture that knows so little of the gospel tradition and its hope for the world, the Church does need to speak about its faith, and priests have a leading role in doing this and enabling it in others. There is no place for reticence when it comes to really good news. Just as we wouldn't hesitate in telling others that a new child has been born into our family, or we've seen a brilliant film, found the best place for a curry, or been on a fantastic holiday, so we should simply and unashamedly tell of what God has done in Jesus Christ. We do not need to be coercive or manipulative or judgemental. We just need to say what the gospel is for us and what it means in our lives. We need to declare its wonderful availability. We need to sing of its tremendous beauty. We need to explain its veracity and its uncomfortable challenges. We need to commend its efficacy. It works. At first that is all you need to say: I received the message and it has made this difference in my life.

As Paul found out in Athens, so it will be today: some will scoff and mock, and others will follow in the way. But many will just want and need to find out more (See Acts 17.32–34). This also is the work of the messenger: to teach and explain the message, to build places for nurture and community so that people can find out. The priest who is a messenger will see this as a vital priority for an evangelising Church. Those who are new to faith or exploring faith or who just want to find out more about faith need a place where they can ask their questions, receive hospitality and begin to catch a glimpse of the Christian faith lived out in the lives of others and in a community of faith. The success of catechumenal models of evangelism like *Alpha* and *Pilgrim*[3] bear witness to the way that this approach to evangelism meets people where they are: not yet ready to come to Church, but willing to give the Christian faith a hearing, and intrigued by the possibilities that the Christian faith declares. This recovery of catechesis as a vital part of ministry must be something that every priest and every church works at more intentionally. This will be true whether you are part of a traditional country church or serving in the most radical fresh expression of church.

This brings us back to that cycle of faith and ministry where in order for it to be declared it must be lived. Our own lives are the best announcement of the gospel.

Your place of replenishing

The question we all need to ask ourselves is: Does the Christian faith work in our life? More specifically, is there a place in our life each day where we are coming back to Christ to find out more; to receive from him, to be replenished by him, a place where we can know our need of God's grace? And is there evidence in our demeanour of the saving beauty of the gospel?

It is this – our receiving from Christ and its confirmation in the life we lead – that will be the heartbeat of priesthood. Through the Holy Spirit and by the grace of Holy Orders, for make no mistake about it, ordination to the priesthood is not some passing out ceremony, not the completion of an apprenticeship year, but a sacramental ministry of grace, whereby the Holy Spirit anoints and equips men and women for a new ministry to make Christ known. It is the particular charism of the priesthood that Christ wishes to be known in and through the ordinary men and women God has called, giving them authority to declare forgiveness, to bless in God's name, and to preside at the Eucharist. The vocation to priesthood is a vocation to represent Christ. The priest, in their own being with all its fears and failings, and in the very frailty of their own faithfulness (and lack of it), is called to be the one who embodies the message of the gospel. This must be renewed in them each day through a disciplined dedication to prayer and the reading of Scripture.

For most clergy the particular joy of the priestly ministry will find its greatest expression, both in what they present to the world and in what they receive from Christ, when they preside at the Eucharist. This has got nothing to do with church tradition; there are just as many evangelicals as catholics who find that it is standing at the table and saying the words that Jesus said on the night before he died and breaking the bread for the people he died to save that is the time when vocation to ordained ministry makes the most sense. It sums up all that priests are called to be, speaking in Jesus' name and inviting people to his table. The Holy Communion is therefore Christ's gift to his Church, the means whereby in the words of the Book of Common Prayer, we declare 'the perpetual memory of his death until his coming again'. It is the glory of the priesthood to preside at the Eucharist. We should never, therefore, forget its evangelistic power. In celebrating the Eucharist, the Church tells the story of God's love, receives the fruits of Christ's victory, and anticipates the banquet of heaven.

In this way, through prayer and contemplation, worship and study, priests and the whole priestly people they serve are formed by the message they bear. They become people of the gospel – messengers who embody the message that was itself embodied in Christ.

Sent into the world

As well as declaring, explaining and embodying the message of Christ, we must also consider the context in which this happens, the world into which we are sent and the particular contexts that make up the parishes and communities where the Church serves.

This is not the time for a long examination of culture or hermeneutics. But it's worth reminding ourselves that for so many people growing up in Britain today, the Church of Jesus Christ is a foreign land and the message of the gospel a foreign tongue. If ever there were an age of itching ears, where people are seduced by all sorts of attractive folly, where there is a teacher for every desire, and where truth is a matter of opinion, it is ours.

It is no good berating the failings of the past or bemoaning the missed opportunities of the present; neither is it simply a matter of shouting louder. If there were an easy solution to evangelising the nation we probably would have found it. Therefore, in the first place, I direct you to the much more demanding and painstaking work of translation. Before people can respond to the gospel they have to hear it and understand it and see it demonstrated as a saving reality. Remember: the Holy Spirit only speaks local dialects. So everyone who wishes to tell the story of Christ must learn the languages of the different cultures of the parishes they serve. We must come alongside people in the networks they inhabit, rather than expecting them to come to us. We must search them out, we must serve them, washing their feet and remembering that as a priest we never stop being a deacon. We must develop new communities of faith and new opportunities for people to hear about and discover faith. We must, as I have already emphasised, demonstrate its usefulness in our own lives and in the life of our communities. And in order to offer a faithful translation we need to know both languages well: the language of the gospel and the language of the culture.

In these ways we will enable people to make the journey into faith, and we will accompany them on the way. This is the real work of evangelism: helping people journey to Christ. Nowadays more people come to Christ on the road to Emmaus than the road to Damascus. Our being a messenger will involve this sort of faithful accompanying; listening to the questions and concerns of those who search and those who weep, sharing the hopes of those who rejoice and helping them all to see and receive Christ.

Such a ministry is profoundly theological. Too often evangelism is seen as the 'shallow end' of faith where enthusiastic people splash around trying to convert others, while the real theologians, asking the really profound and important questions, are down at the deep end. Nothing could be further from the truth. It is as we go about sharing and communicating the gospel that we find out most about it, the refining fire of other people's questions and objections being our greatest school for theological reflection.

Finally, it is not a ministry you do on your own. The Ordinal makes this clear. Ordained ministry is exercised in relationships of ordered accountability. The gospel is much too important and far too precious for anyone to think they can go it alone. That is why priests make the Declaration of Assent. The Church must be sure that its clergy believe the gospel and are committed to the Church. That is why new clergy make the Oath of Canonical Obedience. It is with their bishop and their fellow ministers that they are to exercise this sacred calling. But the Ordinal goes on to say more: it is 'with all God's people' that they 'are to tell the story of God's love'.

It has never been more imperative that we understand ministry as belonging to the whole people of God and of our presbyteral ministry as being one of animation and facilitation. Priests have various responsibilities within the body of the Church; one of them in particular is to enable the ministry of all God's people, encouraging them and equipping them for witness and evangelism. Both those exploring faith, and those called to tell the story of Christ in their own lives (that is, the whole people of God!), need to be taught how to give reasons for the hope they share. One of the chief tasks of ordained ministry will be to teach and to enable this teaching ministry.[4] It has often been neglected in recent years, leaving the Church biblically and theologically undernourished. In other words, the work of catechesis that I mentioned earlier is not just important for those who are exploring faith; those who are already part of the Christian community need to grow in their own faith and discipleship. Every church must be a school for disciples.[5]

Ministry in the Church of England must be ordered, collaborative and accountable. It is not the job of the priest to do all the ministry, but to ensure the ministry is done, encouraging every person to find their part in God's mission of love to the world. This is true for evangelism as it is for every other part of the ministry of the whole people of God.

Nor, as I hope is now apparent, is being a messenger just about preaching. It is about one's whole attitude to ordained ministry. The task is to receive and bear the message of Christ, and this affects and illuminates the whole ministry of the Church. It is what it means to be the apostolic Church – the Church that is sent by God to tell the story of Christ, and to speak of his kingdom.

It will be about preaching though. Preaching is a crucial part of ordained ministry. There is a danger nowadays that some clergy have lost confidence in the medium of preaching. Duped by the notion that people only have a very short attention span, even the idea of standing up and talking to people for more than a couple of minutes seems hopeless. But this is not the case. Look at a stand-up comic. People pay good money to listen to them speak for two hours or more. There are rarely any props, visual aids or PowerPoint presentations. It is just a human being talking. But they are very good at it. They have learned a trade that used to be ours: to speak winningly.

This is another huge topic (and probably the subject of another book!) but let me consolidate a few things that I think are important. First, preachers must have confidence in the power of the spoken word. Preachers must listen to other really good speakers, from whatever walk of life, and learn from them. There is an American saying that is relevant here: 'If they ain't heard it, you ain't said it!' In other words, the brilliance of the content of a sermon is irrelevant if people aren't listening to it. The preacher must learn to be a skilful orator, and this means mastering all the tricks of the oratorical trade.

Secondly, the preacher needs to work at it, and to try different things. It can be very helpful to ask people who you love and trust to offer their unvarnished critique.

Thirdly, preaching and all communication of the gospel message is essentially a spiritual discipline. As Lancelot Andrewes, one-time Bishop of Winchester and member of the team who translated the Bible into what we know of as the King James Version, once wrote:

Let the preacher labour to be heard intelligently, willingly and obediently. And let him not doubt that he will accomplish this rather by the piety of his prayers than by the eloquence of his speech. By praying for himself, and those who he is to address, let him be their beadsman [one who prays for another person] before he becomes their teacher; and approaching God with devotion, let him first raise to him a thirsting heart before he speaks of him with his tongue; that he may speak what he hath been taught and pour out what hath been poured in.[6]

In addition, Evelyn Underhill has written:

> Divine renewal can only come through those whose roots are
> in the world of prayer ... We instantly recognise those services
> and sermons that are the outward expression of the priest's
> interior adherence to God and the selfless love of souls.[7]

The joys of the messenger

I have been a priest for over thirty years. I can honestly say
that the greatest joys of my ministry have been as a messenger.
Occasionally, I have been aware that it is a sermon that has
moved people and that the Holy Spirit has used my preaching
to further his work. But more often than not I have most
been aware of *being a message* in the network of relationships
that make up the day-to-day warp and weft of parish ministry.
I am also aware that very often it has been lay people with
whom I've worked – and very often the newest and least
theologically educated or trained – who have turned out to
be the best, most effective and least self-conscious evangelists.

When you are ordained there are losses as well as gains.
First and foremost, those of us who are ordained lose our
status as gifted amateurs. We may know that it is our love
of the gospel (and nothing much else!) that compelled us
towards ordination, but in the eyes of the world we will
inevitably be seen as the religious professional (and this has
nothing to do with whether you get a stipend or not, but
simply how we are rightly identified as those with power).

Nevertheless, God does use us to tell the story, as well as
require us to lead others, and this is glorious. As I look back
over my years of service, it is people I remember, especially
the people whom I accompanied on the journey into faith.

I remember Peter, saying to me that he couldn't believe in God, though he wanted to, and asking whether it was alright if he came to church, because he liked the sense of community but couldn't in conscience join in many of the words. I told him that of course it was okay, and that his longing for faith *was faith*, even though he couldn't see it at the moment, and that the challenge of his questions, and his deep integrity, was a gift to the Church. And years later – and in his case, it was years later – when he was baptised and confirmed, there was great rejoicing. Great rejoicing in the Church on earth, because we had come to love and value him so much, but also great rejoicing in the Church in heaven, because the gospel tells us that there is 'more joy in heaven over one sinner who repents' (Luke 15.7) than all our so-called righteousness. The theological truth that underpinned and motivated all our evangelism was that Peter was and is greatly loved by God; known by God from the first moment of his being; and that it was for Peter that Christ died. So we do our evangelism not because we want to build the earthly empire of the Church, nor merely snatch lost souls from hell (a rather sad and negative way of approaching something so essentially beautiful and positive), but because we believe that it is the will of God that all people and all things be gathered together in Christ. It is this very good news about God's purposes for all people and for all the world (and therefore for Peter) that we share. Just the remembrance of his story brings me joy.

And I remember Mark, who knocked on the vicarage door a few weeks before I was taking our youth group on pilgrimage, walking from Chichester to Canterbury. He asked whether he could come along. I said he would be very welcome, so long as he joined in with everything we were doing, including the worship, and although I wouldn't expect anyone to say words they didn't believe, he couldn't just go off and do his own thing. He agreed, heartily mocking and forensically dissecting the strange habits of Christianity as we went along; and asking me all sorts of questions that I struggled to answer. But somewhere on the road between Chichester and Canterbury he came to faith in Jesus Christ. His ordination only six or seven years later was another joy. Like the disciples on the Emmaus Road, looking back he found his own heart burning within him. And mine, too, as I tell you about him.

And eighty-year-old Everall, whom I stupidly thought was hostile to the Church because whenever I took Holy Communion to her housebound husband she would quickly withdraw into the kitchen and hardly said a word to me. When he died – three years later and after three years of visits – I went to see her to arrange the funeral. I was nervous about the visit, assuming she took a dim view of faith. I was terribly wrong. She told me how through all those years she had sat in the kitchen with her ear to the wall, joining in the prayers going on in the adjoining room. She thought that because she wasn't confirmed she wasn't allowed to partici-pate. This was my failure to deliver the invitation, my inability to see what was really happening. But God is a Redeemer, and when I apologised to her for my narrow vision, and explained that it was never too late, she too came to the Christ she had always loved, and in the evening of her life was confirmed. Giving her Communion for the first time was a healing for both of us. And no one had told Everall that she wasn't supposed to share the Christian faith. So she happily told others what had happened to her, simply sharing it like the good news it is, and became our church's greatest evangelist.

And there are many others. I didn't convert any of them. That is a holy mystery, the response of the human heart to the sacred heart of Christ. But I had the great privilege of being part of their story, of being a messenger and a witness; and, in turn, helping the Church share and tell its story well. This is the work of priesthood: the priesthood of the whole people of God, making together an offering of prayer and praise, and the particular vocation to lead and teach, and preach and tell, which is the priesthood of the ordained ministry.

As a sign of this vocation, immediately after the Ordination Prayer a new priest is presented with a Bible. The bishop says these words: 'Receive this book as a sign of the authority given you this day to preach the gospel of Christ and minister his holy sacraments.'[8] The Bible represents the teaching authority of the church that the priest holds as guardian of the faith. But it is also evangelistic. These are the words of hope the priest is called to share.

Therefore, the priest must do the work of an evangelist. It is what the Scriptures tell us. It is what the Church needs. It is what the world cries out for, what the human heart craves. It is what I am calling the heartbeat of ministry – to receive the message of Christ, to let Christ tell you again, new every morning, that you are his beloved, that those who are ordained are ordained because of his call, and that the God who calls also sustains in this impossibly beautiful ministry that is only possible because it is God's and not our own. And then to pass it on to others, to share and tell the wonderful story of Jesus Christ. So the priest must proclaim the message; be persistent whether the time is favourable or unfavourable; convince, rebuke, and encourage, all with the utmost patience and with the utmost love.

CHAPTER FIVE

Sentinel

You shall be a crown of beauty in the hand of the Lord,
and a royal diadem in the hand of your God ...
Upon your walls, O Jerusalem,
I have posted sentinels;
all day and all night
they shall never be silent.

ISAIAH 62.3, 6

Isaiah is speaking here about God's great love for his people, of his forgiveness and of God's delight in the covenant he has made. He uses the image of a sentinel, posted upon the walls of Jerusalem, announcing the good news of all that God has done.

We saw in the previous chapter how the Declaration that is made at every ordination service in the Church of England describes the work of a priest and it is worth repeating that:

'they are to proclaim the word of the Lord and to watch for the signs of God's new creation. They are to be messengers, sentinels and stewards of the Lord; they are to teach and admonish, to feed and provide for his family, to search for his children in the wilderness of this world's temptations, and to guide them through its confusions, that they may be saved through Christ for ever.[1]

83

Each of these words – 'messenger', 'sentinel', 'steward' – is rich with meaning. In this chapter I want to focus on what it means to be a sentinel. Of all the terms we are looking at in this book, it is probably the most challenging and the one that is written about the least. Hence this chapter will be a little longer than the others.

So, what is a sentinel? The job of a sentinel is to scan the horizon. To look. To discern. To see what is coming. To interpret. To guide. To announce. To warn.

The word 'sentinel' in the Old Testament

There are thirty-six references to the word 'sentinel' in the Old Testament. At first sight the meaning is clear: a sentinel is one who watches, 'one who keeps vigil'.[2] A sentinel has a regulated responsibility to guard and watch over. The word is used in a variety of ways, however, and this leads to a textured and challenging set of interpretations. It is not insignificant that the most important references are in the prophets, particularly Isaiah and Ezekiel, who see themselves as sentinels. This creates a rich and fascinating hermeneutical connection between sentinel and prophet.

A sentinel could be a keeper of the gate, or a sentry. A sentinel could be guarding the city, or an army encampment, or a particular person, or the fields, especially during harvest, or the community's animals. So in 2 Samuel 18.24–7 a sentinel is posted on the roof of the gate by the wall and reports what he sees to David. In the Song of Solomon 5.7 one of the lovers in the poem is found by the sentinels while they are doing their rounds of the city. In 2 Kings 9.17 a sentinel 'standing on a tower' spies the company of Jehu arriving. In Jeremiah 51.12 as the city is under siege the cry goes up to 'post sentinels'. In

2 Chronicles 20.24 Judah climbs a watchtower and surveys the devastation that is left after battle has concluded and the many corpses lying on the ground. In Job 7.20 God himself is described as 'a watcher of humanity'. In Psalm 127.1 the psalmist makes it clear that no amount of watchtowers and sentries will do any good 'unless the Lord guards the city'. There are other references in the psalms to God guarding people (e.g. Psalm 97.20 or Psalm 121.2, 5) but this is the strongest statement of God being the one who watches and cares, the one who builds and sustains.

The prophets as sentinels of the Lord

Supremely, it is the prophets who not only speak of the God who is a sentinel watching over us, but who are themselves sentinels of the Lord, watching over God's people and speaking about what they see and hear of God. 'The prophet is a sentinel for my God' declares Hosea (Hosea 9.8). 'I raised up sentinels for you' asserts Jeremiah (Jeremiah 6.17). Moreover, it is Jeremiah who claims that the divine task itself is to watch. Looking forward to the return of God's people from exile, God says, through Jeremiah, that 'just as I have watched over them to pluck up and break down, to overthrow, destroy, and bring evil, *so I will watch over them to build and plant*' (Jeremiah 31.27–8). It is the same imagery as Psalm 127. In fact, right at the very beginning of the book of Jeremiah we find images of watching. The prophets are the ones who are able to see what others don't see and make the necessary connection with the activity of God in the life of the world. For God is also watching. Jeremiah uses a striking image to describe this: God is watching with the same patient, focused concentration of a leopard ready to strike (see Jeremiah 5.6).

Jeremiah is called to see and announce with the same

attentive deliberation. He sees God at work in human history and the events of the world. He sees the destruction and disaster that is coming from the north. He is commissioned to be the one who announces this news of foreboding to the people. He explains to them why this calamity is coming upon them and pleads with them to amend their ways. The task of looking and watching therefore also requires interpretation. It leads inexorably to announcing and explaining. This is the task of the sentinel. It is a prophetic and a contemplative task. It requires patience and imagination, and, as we see in the prophets and know from experience of ministry in dark and difficult places, nerves of steel as well.

However, it is Isaiah and Ezekiel who have the most to say to us about the relevance of the work of a sentinel. In what is sometimes called First Isaiah (that is, those oracles spoken by Isaiah in Jerusalem over a period of about forty years from 740–722 BC and prior to the fall of the northern Kingdom of Israel to the Assyrians), Isaiah proclaims:

> For thus the Lord said to me:
> 'Go post a lookout [sentinel],
> let him announce what he sees.'
>
> ISAIAH 21.6

And then a little later on:

> Upon a watchtower I stand, O Lord,
> continually by day,
> and at my post I am stationed
> throughout the night.
>
> ISAIAH 21.8

Isaiah clearly sees his role as a prophet to be one who watches day and night and who announces what he sees and hears.

The sentinel is the one who looks and watches, the one who listens diligently (Isaiah 21.7); but the sentinel is also the one who interprets historical events both inside and outside of history, seeing in them the outworking of God's purposes. In other words, we see again that the sentinel doesn't just announce what is happening but *interprets its meaning*.

Sentinels are mentioned again in Isaiah 52 in a famously beautiful and much-quoted passage. Now the sentinel whom we have seen previously as the one who warns of danger, who calls upon the people to repent and change, who interprets the events of the world in the light of God's purposes, is the one who announces peace and salvation, for God is coming in victory:

> How beautiful on the mountains
> are the feet of the messenger who announces peace,
> who brings good news,
> who announces salvation,
> who says to Zion, 'Your God reigns.'
> Listen! Your sentinels lift up their voices,
> together they sing for joy;
> for in plain sight they see
> the return of the Lord to Zion.
> Break forth together into singing,
> you ruins of Jerusalem;
> for the Lord has comforted his people,
> he has redeemed Jerusalem.

ISAIAH 52.7–9

There is a nice irony here. We are about to be reminded that Jerusalem is in ruins (Isaiah 52.9); nevertheless, it is instructed to break forth into singing! Since it is highly unlikely that anyone would post sentinels on a ruin, these sentinels must be both the prophets who have eyes to see what God is doing and who *act as sentinels* who on hearing the news of victory lead the rejoicing.

Finally, there are two other places in Isaiah worth noting where sentinels are mentioned. First, the rulers of Israel are described as being like blind sentinels, 'without knowledge; they are all silent dogs that cannot bark' (Isaiah 56.10). This identifies those in authority as having the responsibility of a sentinel. It also draws attention to what happens when a sentinel fails in their duty: calamity befalls the people, the righteous perish.

Secondly, in those final chapters of Isaiah where Israel is vindicated and her fortunes restored, and where Israel is described as a 'royal diadem in the hand of your God' (Isaiah 62.3), God's everlasting protection is announced by this proclamation:

Upon your walls, O Jerusalem,
I have posted sentinels;
all day and all night
they shall never be silent.

ISAIAH 62.6

The one who has watched and seen must now declare.

Ezekiel also describes himself as a sentinel. Following the extraordinary and evocative visions that accompany his call, Ezekiel is marooned among exiles and sits with them, stunned and silent, for seven days. The word of the Lord then comes

88

to him declaring: 'Mortal, I have made you a sentinel for the house of Israel; whenever you hear a word from my mouth, you shall give them warning from me' (Ezekiel 3.17).

However, there is a painful paradox for Ezekiel: no sooner has he received the call to be God's sentinel than God commands him to shut himself in his house (Ezekiel 3.24). God says that he will make his tongue cling to the roof of his mouth so that 'you shall be speechless and unable to reprove them' (Ezekiel 3.26), thus creating an impossible situation: called to be a sentinel, yet commanded to be silent, though God promises that on the day he is needed his mouth shall be opened (see Ezekiel 24.25–7).

This brief examination of the term 'sentinel' leads us to conclude that sentinels are appointed by God. They are called to watch and listen. They are called to announce and explain. They are called to interpret. They are called to lead the rejoicing as well as sound the warning. They are called to speak truth to power, no matter how uncomfortable. They are personally responsible and responsible to God.

How much of this was in Cranmer's mind when he included this word in the Ordinal we do not know. This vocation, however, which we can now see clearly is both prophetic and contemplative, theological and evangelistic, is close to the heart of priestly vocation and is an element in priestly formation and ministry that needs, urgently, to be recovered.

References to watching and listening in the New Testament

Although there is no specific reference to 'sentinel' in the New Testament, there are several passages that speak of *watching* and *listening*.

'Blessed are your eyes, for they see, and your ears, for they hear' says Jesus to his disciples. 'Truly I tell you, many prophets and righteous people longed to see what you see, but did not see it, and to hear what you hear and did not hear it' (Matthew 13.16). Jesus is, of course, referring to the very prophets whose ministry we have just been exploring. In Jesus, God has come to vindicate his people and reveal his purpose in a unique way. Now the disciples see and hear things that the prophets longed for. They have an intimacy with God that was spoken of, glimpsed, but never fulfilled until the coming of Christ.

The context of these words is Jesus' discussion on the meaning of parables after he had told the parable of the sower (Matthew 13.1–17). 'Why do you speak in parables?' the disciples ask (Matthew 13.10). Jesus replies:

> To you it has been given to know the secrets of the kingdom of heaven ... I speak to them in parables so that 'seeing they do not perceive, and hearing they do not listen, nor do they understand.' With them indeed is fulfilled the prophecy of Isaiah that says: 'You will listen, but never understand, and you will indeed look, but never perceive. For this people's heart has grown dull, and their ears are hard of hearing, and they have shut their eyes; so that they might not look with their eyes and listen with their ears ...'
>
> MATTHEW 13.10–15

Then Jesus says, 'But blessed are your eyes, for they see' (Matthew 13.16).

Jesus is not quite calling them sentinels, but the connection is clear. This quotation from Isaiah, which comes immediately after he has received his vocation to be the one sent by God

(Isaiah 6.9), illustrates the distance from God that the people have travelled. They look and listen but they do not hear or comprehend. And when the disciples fail to understand the meaning of the feeding miracles Jesus rebukes them saying, 'Do you have eyes, but fail to see? Do you have ears, and fail to hear? And do you not remember?' (Mark 8.18).

Similarly, in the little apocalypse of Mark 13, a theme explored in some of Paul's writings,[3] the disciples are told of the necessity of watchfulness: they must 'keep alert' and 'stay awake' (Mark 13.32–7). Some of this looks forward to Christ's return but could equally be understood as a way of alerting the disciples to the manner in which they must now inhabit the earth, looking out for the signs of God's kingdom and communicating this to others. Indeed, Mark 13.37, which the NRSV translates as 'keep awake', could just as accurately be translated as 'watch'; and in the Revelation to John, each message to the seven churches ends with the injunction: 'Let anyone who has an ear listen to what the Spirit is saying to the churches' (Revelation 2.7).

Finally, when Luke tells the story of the disciples on the Emmaus Road, he constructs this narrative around two dramatic injunctions of God. First, we are told, when they met Jesus on the road 'their eyes were kept from recognising him' (Luke 24.16). Then, when they do recognise him in the breaking of bread, 'their eyes were opened' (Luke 24.31).[4]

Somehow God is at work in both the closing and the opening of their eyes. The sentinel is one who has had their eyes opened by God, the one who is able to see and know Jesus intimately, in the breaking open of the Word and in the breaking of the bread. This person is turned around and is called to announce (communicate) this news to others, who, in turn, have their eyes opened too.

This is the ministry that priests take on: 'To watch for the signs of God's new creation.'[5]

'Sentinel' in the writings of the early Church

Writing in the fourth century, several of Augustine of Hippo's sermons reflect on issues of leadership. In his sermon on Psalm 127, Augustine specifically talks about the Christian leader as a sentinel. He assumes the city mentioned in the psalm is Jerusalem. But he also points out that the 'house of God is a city' and that this house is 'the people of God';[6] just as 'she has builders, labouring at her building up, so also she has guards (sentinels)'. Referencing the ministry of the apostle Paul and his words at 2 Corinthians 11.3 about resisting temptation and having a 'sincere and pure devotion to Christ', Augustine observes that this 'guardianship' is the work of a bishop. With the utmost of their power, bishops are to keep watch over those to whom they are sent. Then using the image of a watchtower he says that 'just as a higher place is assigned to the vinedresser in charge of the vineyard, so also to the bishops a more exalted station is allotted'. This exaltation has nothing to do with status though. It is the high vantage point from which things can be seen clearly. It also requires single-minded reliance upon God:

A perilous account is rendered of this high station, except we stand here with a heart that causes us to stand beneath (God's) feet in humility, and pray ... that he who knows your minds may be Himself your keeper ... We are watchful on our guard, but vain on our watchfulness, except He who sees your thoughts guards you. He keeps guard while you are awake; He keeps guard also while you are asleep.[7]

Interestingly, Augustine then employs two of the other words
that so struck Cranmer:

> For we guard you in our office of *stewards*; but we wish to
> be guarded together with you. We are as it were *shepherds*
> unto you; but beneath that Shepherd we are fellow sheep
> with you. We are as it were your teachers from this station;
> but beneath Him, the One Master, we are school fellows
> with you in this school [my italics].[8]

The Christian minister as sentinel is one who watches over
and guards the Church, but also one who is under the watchful
guardianship of God and is looking as much to God as to
the people; indeed, is one who cannot watch out for the
people unless looking to God.

Writing to the church in Nicomedia, a wealthy and influential city in the eastern half of the Roman Empire at about
the same time, Gregory of Nyssa, another great teacher of
the early Church, advised them on the selection of a new
bishop, by saying that they should not look for someone with
wealth or connections, but someone who had 'a single eye
to the things of God'.[9] This is another way of saying that
the bishop needs to be a sentinel, one who looks for the
things of God and for the activity of God.

Then, in a most striking phrase, Gregory remarks that
what the Church needs is fresh spring water, even if it flows
through a wooden pipe.[10] Augustine comments in the sermon
on Psalm 127: 'If we wish to be guarded by Him who was
humble for our sakes, and who was exalted to keep us, let us
be humble.'[11] The sentinel is one who is humble and obedient
to their vocation to watch and to be watched over. They are
not the living water, but the pipe through which it flows.

Writing a couple of centuries later, another great teacher of the faith, Gregory the Great, also drew on the notion of God's minister as sentinel: 'A sentinel always selects a high vantage point in order to be able to observe things better. In the same way, whoever is appointed as a sentinel for a people should live on the heights so that he can help his people by having a broad perspective.'[12] But he goes on, reflecting painfully on his own fallings as a minister:

> I find it hard to make such a statement because such words are a reproach to myself. My preaching is mediocre, and my life does not cohere with the values I preach so inadequately. I do not deny that I am guilty, for I recognise in myself lethargy and negligence.[13]

The minister who is sentinel, then, must look at their own heart with an unyielding honesty.

To our previous conclusions about the ministry of sentinel as found in Scripture we can now add that a sentinel is called to live on the heights (placing themselves in positions where they can see clearly); and a sentinel is under the watchful guardianship of God. The calling is, therefore, about seeing God as well as being seen by God. As Christopher Beeley has commented in his book about leadership in the early Church:

> Far above any particular skill or expertise, even more important than education or management technique, the most crucial pre-requisite for church leadership is the pastor's holiness and life in Christ. Whatever other skills we may bring to pastoral ministry God will no doubt use in surprising ways, but it is our life in Christ that makes for effective ministry.[14]

It is nurturing this life in Christ that is also the work of the sentinel. What does it mean for today?

Being a sentinel in the Church today

Our examination of the biblical material shows that the fundamental vocation of the sentinel is to look. Sentinels stand on towers and scan horizons. All sorts of other things flow from this. But let us start by identifying what horizons we are talking about.

The first, and most obvious horizon, is God. The priest who is a sentinel will be a person of prayer, someone who makes space for God to be God.[15] God will be their delight, the focus of their attention and the source of their energy and motivation. They will seek out places where God can be encountered and considered. In this way, we are only properly empowered when we stop trying to set the agenda ourselves.

The spiritual discipline that fuels this is contemplation which can take many forms. Contemplation can be the quiet attentiveness of a Quaker meeting; Evensong in an Anglican Cathedral; the footfall of a pilgrimage to Santiago; or the pulsing music of charismatic tongues.[16] What always happens is that space is made for God. We look at God and listen to God. This requires discipline as well as desire and a personal commitment to wait upon the divine will and the divine presence.[17]

The practice of contemplation is transformative. Sarah Coakley describes it as 'a special form of "vulnerability"' which is 'not an invitation to be battered; nor is its silence a silencing … by choosing to make a space in this way, one "practises the presence of God" – the subtle enabling presence of a God who neither shouts nor obliterates.'[18] Conversely it is the simplest thing in the world *not* to contemplate. The world, just as much as the Church, is imperilled by such unreflective leadership, and by those who only look at what they want to see.

Contemplative prayer isn't easy. Each person needs to find the way of making space for God that nurtures them in their vocation and ministry. Gabbling all our stuff to God, and telling God our agenda for the world (and our parish in particular) – or worse still not praying at all except when we are leading worship in church – is much easier.

But the prayer that is the heart and summit of all prayer, which is contemplative, which is that 'ardent desire to dwell in God's presence, to listen to God's voice, to look at God's beauty, to touch God's incarnate Word and to taste fully God's infinite goodness',[19] that waiting in the presence of God, asking that God might shape our minds and our will is, as we have discovered, a bit like standing on a watch-tower.

The second horizon is the world; both the big cultural and political issues of the day and the local and particular issues of the context and community in which each priest serves. In his influential book *The Prophetic Imagination*, Walter Brueggemann speaks about what forms our consciousness and worldview, and whether we have been 'robbed of the courage or power to think an alternative thought'.[20] Before any new vision can be implemented it has to be imagined.

Brueggemann says that our culture is 'competent to implement almost anything and to imagine almost nothing'; it is, therefore, the 'vocation of the prophet' – and the sentinel – 'to keep alive the ministry of imagination, to keep on conjuring and proposing alternative futures to the single one' that (those in power) urge as the only ones thinkable.[21]

Sentinels speak truth to power

The sentinel therefore speaks truth to power. The sentinel must speak clearly, imaginatively and fearlessly on the big issues that are upon us and those coming towards us, presenting God's perspective, demonstrating God's care and, where necessary, announcing God's verdict: issues such as the global catastrophe of climate change; our obsession with cheap petrol (or strawberries!) all the year round; the widening gap between rich and poor; the easy accessibility of pornography and alcohol and their reprehensible effects upon the young in particular; the degrading and objectifying of women; the sexualisation of children; the shocking dependency of much of our economy on selling arms; the renewal of our nuclear capability while at the same time lecturing others on the reasons they shouldn't have such weapons themselves; our demonisation of immigrants; our tolerance of casual racism; the shocking indifference of unregulated markets and financial institutions, and the damage this has done not just to our economy, but in our confidence in the systems that form and shape our nation. And more besides. The world is not as God would wish it. The sentinel is the one who looks: the contemplative. The sentinel is the one who *having looked* interprets and declares: the prophetic.

In his most recent book, Brueggemann argues that this imagining of new futures also requires the prophet (and the Church) to speak out. Echoing Coakley's phrase that 'silence does not mean silencing', he contrasts the silence that is making space for God, even awe before the presence of God, to that oppressive silence where the dominant voices of vested interest silence opposition and debate. There is too much of the second sort of silence in the world, and not enough of the first. However, the sentinel watches and listens silently *in order to speak*. Brueggemann cites the example of Martin Luther King Jr speaking out about the war in Vietnam in 1967, in a talk entitled, 'Beyond Vietnam: A Time to Break the Silence'.[22]

By announcing, explaining and interpreting the sentinel speaks prophetically into the issues and concerns of the world. The sentinel *breaks* the silence of oppression, ignorance and apathy. They also speak *out* of a silent watching and waiting upon God. Their ability to see things that others don't see and comment and interpret in new and imaginative ways flows from the time given to looking at God and brooding on God's word. Sentinels scan the horizon of the world and seek to understand its moods and motivations *from the perspective of God*, even to look at the world with God's eyes. It is precisely this way of looking that we saw in Jeremiah, Isaiah and Ezekiel; and also mirrored in Christ.

Contemplation, and therefore the ministry of the sentinel, is not some escapist hankering after religious experience, and certainly not a way of avoiding looking at the world. Quite the opposite. Rowan Williams argues this brilliantly in his hugely significant address to the Thirteenth Ordinary Assembly of the Catholic Synod of Bishops. Citing the example of Dietrich Bonhoeffer, he shows how true prayer purifies our motives and leads to a hungering and thirsting after true righteousness, leading to prophetic action and what Brueggemann calls a reimagining of the future. Speaking about evangelisation in particular, Williams notes that this can never be separate from contemplation, that evangelism – and, I suppose, all ministry – 'is always an overflow of something else'.[23]

Through contemplation we reimagine the whole world and see it through the lens of the God who delights in looking at us and coming to us in Christ. Williams therefore says that the silent gazing on God, and looking at the world in this way, is the goal of discipleship. Elsewhere Williams even writes that 'doctrine is a waste of time' unless it leads to contemplation.[24]

Therefore, remembering Gregory the Great's and Augustine's injunction that those who are appointed sentinel should 'live on the heights and have a broad perspective', we need to ask: What are we looking at? What is our perspective? What demands attention? And what is it we choose to ignore?

The sentinel looks for what is coming, discerns its meaning and leads the people in their lament or joy: as the Ordinal puts it, watches 'for the signs of God's new creation'.[25] It is not an easy vocation. Most of the time it won't look very useful at all. You stand on the tower. You gaze into the distance. You watch for movement. You fight off the boredom. You try to concentrate. You wait for the moment when something happens. You endure the many moments when it doesn't.

What is the practical outworking of this for today?

At his farewell service as Bishop of Sheffield, Bishop Jack Nicholls observed:

> Priests are not essentially teachers, preachers, pastors, leaders, prophets, strategists or managers, though they may be called to be any or all of these. Priests are justified only by their being and their seeing; by standing in that place which holds the stars and the gutter with a joyful heart for the praise of God and a big capacious heart for the pain of the world. There is no other place to stand for a priest.[26]

Such 'being' and 'seeing' are the call of the sentinel. As we have seen, it begins with prayer, making space for God and learning how to see the world from God's perspective.

The call also means sometimes having to share unwelcome truths. This is hard enough in itself but if it is what you are called and compelled to do, then how do you maintain trust-worthiness, especially in the face of criticism and opposition? Rowan Williams says that it is to do with consistency and patience, the 'willingness to stick with a situation of dis-ease and conflict and not look for a quick and false solution'.[27]

This brings us back to those disciplines of faithfulness – the ability to wait and watch – that are distinctive of one who is a sentinel, a rhythm of prayer and study marked by patience, persistence and a 'healthy scepticism about hasty expectations'.[28] There is an important and unsettling paradox here. It is the person who is unafraid of silence (the person who has stood on the watchtower, be that watchtower a street corner or an empty church each morning) who is most able to speak. Like the prophets who also saw and interpreted, the process will often be uncomfortable but it will carry great authority. Alternatively, if we don't watch and wait, if our horizons diminish, then our speech will be babble, lacking either authenticity or even plausibility. A sentinel is trusted because, however unwelcome the message, they are known to be someone who consistently says what they see to be true, who is not so hasty as to speak before there is some clarity about what is being encountered. A second paradox is that the one who spends time looking at God is also the one, as we saw with the prophets, who allows God to look at them.

There is a cost to this ministry. Sentinels must have the courage to wait. Many sophisticated detractors hanker after quick and easy answers. That is the nature of the culture we inhabit. Social media demands an endless stream of sound-bites, not the deep waters of considered reflection. When things are seen, though, and when the poetic and prophetic imagination begins to see *what* they mean and *where* they lead, further courage is required: to announce what we see, and to announce it clearly. This is the hard and lonely aspect of any vocation to lead. We know how offensive and unwelcome the poetic oracles spoken by the prophets were. We saw their 'immense courage and imagination'[29] We recall Isaiah's warning against being those who fail in this regard: 'Israel's sentinels are blind … they are all silent dogs that cannot bark' (Isaiah 56.10). Jeremiah (and other prophets) were considered traitors.[30]

This aspect of the sentinel's vocation leads to another difficult issue for clergy: whose affirmation are we seeking – God's or the congregation's? Or to put it another way: do we end up announcing what we see, or what we think people want to hear? Both the Scriptures themselves and early Church tradition had a lot to say on this sensitive subject. Gregory the Great wrote:

> The mind of the priest is often seduced by the approval of those below him, and consequently he is exalted beyond himself. While he is outwardly surrounded with immense favour, internally he becomes empty of the truth. Forgetful of how he is, he scatters himself among the voices of others and believes what he hears all around him rather than what he should discern about himself from within.[31]

St Paul, also recognising this problem, says to the Church in Galatia: 'If I were still pleasing people, I would not be a servant of Christ' (Galatians 1.10); and to the church in

Thessalonica: 'We speak not to please mortals, but to please God' (1 Thessalonians 2.4). Which is not to say we should shun the approval and the praise of others, but be very wary of letting it become our motivation.

Christian leaders can't stop people admiring them, offering praise, or even following them, nor should they try to. It would be too confusing. In this regard, their salvation rests upon being sure that they are following Christ, and seeking his affirmation, not their own. St Paul's advice to the vain and confused church in Corinth is pertinent: 'Be imitators of me, as I am of Christ' (1 Corinthians 11.1). Nevertheless, it could be said that the whole of Gregory the Great's Pastoral Rule is aimed at 'driving church leaders back from the precipice of their own ambition'[32] Indeed, Gregory the Great ruminated:

> What kind of sentinel am I? I do not stand on the pinnacle of achievement; I languish in the pit of my frailty. And although I am unworthy, the creator and redeemer of us all has given me grace to see life whole and an ability to speak effectively of it.[33]

As I look back over my ordained ministry I realise that it is this part that I have found hardest. I have often craved praise and looked for affirmation in the wrong places. But I also know that on those occasions when I have been most faithful to the truth as I have seen it through the lens of Christ, I have been most fulfilled.

In his poem 'Why Do You Stay Up So Late?' Don Paterson offers what, for me, is a very priestly picture of humanity. The first stanza addresses the question of the poem's title. The poet recalls a happy day spent at the beach with his interlocutor where they collected stones, and in order to decide which ones to keep and take home, 'played the jeweller' and plunged them into a rock pool to discover which ones 'would blink the secret colour/it had locked up somewhere in its stony sleep'.[34]

In the second stanza we find the poet sitting up late each night, 'collecting the dull things of the day' in which there might be 'some possibility'. But now there is no rock pool to help, so he concludes:

> ... I look at them and look at them until
> One thing makes a mirror in my eyes
> Then I paint it with a tear to make it bright.
> That is why I sit up through the night.[35]

This is someone looking at the world as a sentinel. Looking closely and carefully. Entering into the pain and the joy of a situation. Finding an exalted position, that as Augustine and Gregory the Great insisted, is not about status, but about being able to see clearly. It is what priests are called to do. It involves our weeping as well as our rejoicing. It is contemplative and prophetic. It requires seeing things as they are and as they could be. However, it is among the hardest and loneliest aspects of priestly ministry. It is certainly not a pathway to worldly success. The world, and even the people we serve, will misunderstand and not necessarily like nor heed the sound of our trumpet. They will think we are blowing our own, not God's. All priests must be constantly alert to this danger, working collegially with lay and ordained colleagues, testing their assumptions and conclusions against the yardstick of Scripture and the accumulated wisdom of tradition. (This is why the Ordinal calls a priest steward as well as sentinel and messenger.)[36] Despite this, and the opposition that certainly comes when the gospel gets under the skin, there is joy.

Isaiah told us that the feet of the messenger who brings good news are lovely (Isaiah 52.7). The sentinels lift their voices in praise (Isaiah 52.8). Through the prayerful perseverance of tears, the true colour and the joy of a situation or a person is discovered. The process contains the deepest truth of the ordained vocation. After all, what greater joy can there be than to tell the story of God's love revealed in Christ? What greater joy than to preside at the Eucharist and be the mouth that speaks the words of God, the hands that deliver nourishment and blessing to God's people? What greater joy than to be the channel through which God's forgiveness is passed from sinner to sinner, and to sit with those whose burdens are laid at the cross? What greater joy than to stand alongside our sisters and brothers at the times of their brightest delight and their darkest sorrow? What greater joy than the calling to look upon God and look upon the world and share with others the things we see, knowing that we too, with them, are held in the watchful gaze of God?

This is the joy of the priesthood, at font and at altar, in pulpit and at school gate, in the crematorium, the hospital, the work canteen and the local pub, at deathbed and at crib; and it will be multiplied, expanded and transformed by the discipline of watchful prayer that requires us to be sentinels of the Lord, to take our place upon the watchtowers and to look. First of all, for God, for we are called to a prayer-filled ministry of word and of sacrament: as the psalmist said: 'Unless the Lord guards the city, the guard keeps watch in vain' (Psalm 127.1); without this foundation all our anxious toil, our getting up early, our late-night e-mails, our feverish desire to be liked and to be successful, will be to no avail. But then to the world. As the prophet Ezekiel spoke the very words of God, so we speak God's words of invitation and challenge to the communities we serve (see Ezekiel 33.7). Then the Church can be the 'space cleared by God through Jesus in which people ... become what God made them to be ... a place where we can see properly'.[37]

Unfortunately, the contemporary Church of England, and I suppose other churches as well, have not had eyes to see or ears to hear this vital element in ordained ministry, and yet it is there in the Ordinal waiting to be recovered. A greater and more conscious emphasis on the ordained minister as sentinel, and an encouragement to develop the disciplines that undergird it, may deepen our dependence on God and our willingness to watch and wait upon God and to stand in uncomfortable places in the ways we saw exemplified in the lives of the prophets. And because the contemplative has been neglected, we shouldn't be surprised that our prophetic witness has been blunted.

Reclaiming the language of sentinel and all that goes with it could be enormously fruitful and liberating for ordained ministry, helpfully counterbalancing some of the more managerial and target-driven models of leadership. Let our key performance indicator be this: time spent looking at God and looking at the world.

CHAPTER SIX

Steward

Think of us in this way, as servants of Christ and stewards
of God's mysteries. Moreover, it is required of stewards
that they should be found trustworthy.

1 CORINTHIANS 4.1–2

I want to speak in this chapter about what it means for a
priest to be a trustworthy steward of the mysteries of God,
which is both the treasure of the gospel and the people of
God whose character and vocation is also priestly. As we have
seem, the Ordinal charges priests to 'feed and provide for
God's family ... guided by the Spirit, they are to discern and
foster the gifts of all God's people, that the whole Church
may be built up in unity and faith'.[1]

The great composer Bruckner never completed his ninth
symphony. It was to be the summation of his life's work, but
he died in 1896 before it was finished. The first three movements were written, but only fragments and sketches of the
fourth movement remained. He told friends that the symphony
was to culminate in a triumphant 'Alleluia', and was to be a
hymn of praise to God. Indeed, the whole symphony carried
the dedication *Dem lieben Gott*: 'To dearest God'. These
same friends and colleagues found piles of papers that were

the beginnings of this fourth movement. They discovered some passages that had been fully orchestrated, but of the crucial finale, they found nothing.

Most orchestras, performing this work, usually play the first three movements only. Several composers over the years have pieced together a fourth movement from what remains. However, if there were to be a serious attempt to construct the missing movement what would be the best way to do it? Would we just ask one person? Or wouldn't it be better to gather together an experienced group of musicians, scholars and conductors who loved Bruckner's music, and knew it intimately, and approach them? They would then completely immerse themselves in the first three movements, and remaining faithful to them, and from their knowledge of Bruckner, produce the fourth. This fourth movement would be consistent with what is already written, but at the same time entirely new.

The symphony of God's love and the orchestra of the Church

The task facing the Church today is analogous to the writing of this fourth movement. We don't usually notice though. The first three movements are written: they are the unfolding story of God's involvement with the world he has made. You could say the first movement is the Old Testament, telling us how God chooses a people to make his purposes known and demonstrate his goodness. The second and central movement is the story of Christ, God's disclosure of his nature and the story of how God reconciles the world to himself through the death and resurrection of Christ. And the third movement is the outpouring of the Spirit in the life of the Church and for the transformation of the world from Pentecost until yesterday.

But the fourth movement is not yet written. It is the song of God's love for the world today; in order for it to be sung, and so that it can be heard in the culture and circumstances of the different and very varied communities in which the Church serves, God is calling together a band of players, musicians, scholars, conductors – those who play the violin *and* those who play the spoons – and he is asking us to so inhabit the beauty and purposeful melodies and rhythms of the first three movements that we will, for our day, for our parish, for our world, produce the fourth. It will be entirely consistent with what has gone before. It will be startlingly new. Just as the Declaration of Assent made by every priest charges us to 'Proclaim the faith afresh in each generation.'[2]

We have no ministry of our own, no faith of our own. The task of presbyters in the Church of God is to receive, inhabit, pass on, and in so doing write, the fourth movement for the one, holy, catholic and apostolic Church of Jesus Christ. They will lead and order the people of God in the churches where they serve so that they – together and individually – will be able to make a joyful noise unto the Lord, and sing a new song.

The priest as conductor

The task of the priest is not to be the lead player, not the first violin or the concert pianist, but the conductor, harmonising and utilising the gifts and creativity of the whole.[3] When we call a priest a steward, this is what we are referring to: the role of the priest in animating, releasing and directing the gifts of the whole people of God in ministry. The priest is vital to the task of playing the music. Sometimes an individual priest will appear to be very visible: they will wave their arms about and direct the action; sometimes they will even have to pick up the instruments and remind people how they are played, or pick out the basic melody on one finger on the piano so that people get it in their heads. It is so that *others can play* the music, however, that they are called to conduct.

And it is the music that they serve: the beautiful music of the gospel of Christ that is being written and played in and through the great orchestra of his Church. This is why the New Testament itself calls the people of God 'priestly'. It is not because each person is a priest, but because the priesthood of the Church is offered through the different gifts and ministries of the people. One of the very particular roles of the ordained ministry is to make this happen. Or, as I say at most licensing services of new vicars: it is not your job to do all the ministry; it is your job to make sure the ministry is done.

Some clergy balk at this. 'I was not ordained to be a manager' they tell me. Well, actually they were; only the biblical word is 'steward'. It is the term Paul uses to Titus to describe a bishop's ministry (Titus 1.7). All clergy, sharing in the bishop's ministry, or in other non-episcopal denominations sharing in the apostolic ministry of their church, are called to oversee the ministry of the people of God and the work and witness of God's church in the locality where they serve. 1 Peter suggests that the Church itself is a community of stewards who serve each other with the different gifts they have received (see 1 Peter 4.10).

Leading the Church in this way is a spiritual as well as a

theological task. Take the Eucharist itself: presiding at Holy Communion will be the most tangible outward sign of the new ministry God bestows upon those who are ordained. Paul writes, 'For I received from the Lord, what I also handed on to you ...' (1 Corinthians 11.23). These are remarkable words. They indicate that at a very early stage in the development of the Church's liturgy and doctrine some things were considered so precious, so central and so important, that they weren't to be messed around with. And it is worth noting that this was a couple of centuries before the canon of Scripture that is now the New Testament had even been thought about.

Presiding at the Eucharist

'What I receive,' says Paul, 'I faithfully hand on.' Those words 'hand on' are the root of our word 'tradition'. A priest is a steward of this tradition; called to faithfully receive and faithfully pass on: to be trustworthy. Word and sacrament are not theirs to fiddle around with, but to cherish, interpret and deliver. In this way priests are stewards of the very mysteries of the gospel itself, the living presence of Christ through his holy word and through the sacraments of the New Covenant. They are called to hand things over and hand things on, to feed and sustain God's people.

We have introduced a new element into our ordination rite this year. At ordination services in the Chelmsford Diocese, at the Offertory representatives of the parishes where the new priests serve present them with bread and wine – and possibly chalices and patens as well – showing that their ordination to the priesthood is clearly a sacramental ministry as well as a ministry of the word and is done with and on behalf of the people of God. The bishop then says:

'Receive from the Holy People of God the bread and wine, gifts from God to be brought to God's table' and the newly ordained priests then place the bread and wine on the altar. Similarly, in another ordination rite of the Western Church, as the newly ordained priest receives the bread and wine, the bishop declares: 'Understand what you do, imitate what you celebrate, and conform your life to the mystery of the Lord's cross.'[4]

Now let's be clear, none of this has anything to do with any particular church tradition. I don't care if people are 'swinging from the chandeliers charismatics' or 'placing half a dozen chandeliers on the altar' Anglo-Catholics, and nor does God. But what does matter is that standing at the table breaking bread is what priests are called to do and is the clearest possible expression of the ministry to which they have been called, for in imitating what they celebrate they imitate the Lord himself. The fruits of His offering, made once for all upon the cross, are made manifest in our midst and as the bread is taken, blessed, broken and shared, so we ask God – every time we preside at God's table or receive Holy Communion – to fashion us and use us for his purposes, and conform our lives to the mystery of the cross.

As good stewards of the gospel, first and foremost, priests must know their own need of God. They must come to the Lord with empty hands and penitent hearts and find in Jesus balm and solace for their own lives, and fresh resolve to hold his cross high, so that the whole world may be drawn to Christ. And this is what is happening in Holy Communion: we are holding before the Church and proclaiming to the world the saving drama of what God has done in Christ; what we have received is passed on.

It is my hope that every priest thinks about this when they preside at the Holy Communion for the first time; that as they hold the bread and raise the cup, they remember it is the Lord's death that they are setting before the world, even though inevitably first-night nerves probably mean they will be thinking far more about the mechanics of what they are doing and saying. We should never forget, however, as presbyters in the Church of God we are called to imitate Christ's life of self-giving love.

I also want to say that although I have been a priest for over thirty years, I still tremble with awe and wonder every time I stand at the Lord's table. I am overwhelmed by the privilege and honour that God has called me to this ministry. In the words of Thomas Merton:

Day after day I am more and more aware that I am anything but my everyday self at the altar: this consciousness of innocence is really a sense of replacement. I am superseded by one in who I am fully real. Another has taken over my identity (or he has revealed it), and this other is of tremendous infancy. And I stand at the altar ... with my eyes all washed in the light that is eternity and become one who is agelessly reborn.[5]

Priesthood is not a set of clothes that is put on in the morning and taken off when you go to bed, but a new identity that is, for those God is calling, the fulfilling of the baptismal vocation to be clothed in Christ. There are many different ways of being clothed in Christ, but in every case it is about our whole person, never one aspect of it, never something that can be put on or taken off. Of course it will be essential for every priest to develop a healthy balance of prayer, study, service and leisure. That is the life Scripture calls us to. Even on a day off we have not stopped being a minister of the gospel; we are just on those days being a minister who values the gift of Sabbath and lives a biblically ordered life.

Moreover, because the priest has a special vocation within the household of the Church and because that is most evident when we stand at the table as the one who presides, representing the people to Christ and Christ to the people, then we feel different when we say these words and do these things that come to us from Christ. They will come to symbolise the whole of our ministry, which is to lift high the cross of Christ, to feed his people and to enable them to fulfil their vocation as the priestly people of God.

There is a much-neglected, quintessentially English, and probably much-maligned school of pastoral care that has been squeezed out of the Church and the world in the engulfing professionalisation of pretty much everything. When it encounters a problem, large or small, be it a trifling disagreement or a heart-rending tragedy, this approach responds with the advice: let's put the kettle on. Many a disagreement was resolved, hurt healed and wrong righted over a cup of tea.

There may be more that must be done, but there is never less. There is something beautifully human and innately sacramental about such an approach. Hospitality, food and drink, the innate democracy of the table where all sit as equals are things which of themselves and in their own quiet way breed reconciliation and healing.

It is the ministry to which priests are called: to preside at the table; to offer food and drink; to bring people together; to cast down the mighty and lift up the lowly; to become colour blind to difference in the scandalously generous table fellowship of the Lord. It is the work of a steward.

And it goes without saying that Jesus himself was always eating with people. In the end, I suppose, it was what got him killed. 'He eats with tax collectors and sinners'(see Matthew 9.11). That was the charge against him; he never even tried to deny it. We saw him in the brothel last night. Look at his followers: zealots, peasant fisherman, tax collectors.

So as a priest imitates Christ, the person who stewards people; gathers the people of God together, presides at the table and feeds them, two things need to be remembered. First, at the table the priest represents Christ, and, at the same time, and by the power of the Holy Spirit, the bread and wine themselves become vehicles of Christ's presence, for 'whoever eats of this bread will live forever' (John 6.51).

Secondly, the table of the Lord is to be set in the midst of the world. While our Eucharist will usually take place in church, as I look back over my ministry it is the times we have taken the Eucharist out of the church building that have been the most memorable. I have, for instance, cele-brated the Eucharist outside the gates of Faslane; by the side of the road with a tin cup and a plastic plate with a group of pilgrims on our way to Walsingham; and more recently in the Holy Land outside Bethlehem in the fields where shepherds would have watched over their sheep and angels sang of peace on earth; and at the deathbed of a faithful servant of Christ.

So let us never forget the evangelistic power of worship and of the Eucharist in particular. In celebrating the Eucharist the Church tells the story of God's love, receives the fruits of Christ's victory, and anticipates the banquet of heaven. Therefore the one who presides must also be the one who invites. In fact, our entire ministry should be motivated by the knowledge that Christ has gone before us and prepared a place for us. He asks us, as ministers of his gospel, endlessly to hand out the invitations to the banquet of heaven of which the Eucharist is a shadow.

A table set

'You prepare a table before me in the presence of my enemies' says Psalm 23 (v 5). What, exactly, does this mean?

Does it mean our enemies look upon us while we feast; their noses pressed to the glass as we toast ourselves with champagne and gorge ourselves on the finest fare? Or does it mean, literally, in the midst of the horrors of the world and in the difficulties and challenges of the very particular parishes where we serve now and where we will serve in the future, and wherever there is hurt and disappointment, tragedy and grief, we are called to set before the world the death and resurrection of Christ and with it the feast whereby the fruits of that sacrifice are made known?

In the sort of tradition in which my faith and vocation were formed, celebrating Holy Communion for the first time was akin to the consummation of a marriage. The Ordination Service was one thing, but what was really looked forward to was presiding at the Eucharist for the first time.

Elaborate plans were made for my first Mass.[6] Music chosen. Servers rehearsed. However, as I started to sing the preface of the Eucharistic Prayer, a very small child in the front couple of rows of the church started to scream loudly and painfully in the way only very small children can. She was completely inconsolable. At first, I am embarrassed to say, I was slightly irritated. My first Mass was being spoiled. But then – thankfully – I came to my senses. For the Eucharist does not belong to me. Just as we shouldn't refer to any service as 'mine', so we should also avoid speaking about 'my church'. The Church belongs to Christ. It is his body, and we are its servants and stewards. I, for instance, always try to refer to 'the diocese I serve' not 'my diocese'.

The Eucharist is Christ's gift to the Church, a 'perpetual memory of that his precious death until his coming again'.[7] And what is the Eucharist for – indeed what is the point of the whole Christian faith – if not the meeting place between the pain and sorrow of the world and the good news of God's reconciling love in Christ? It is the place where we learn to love our enemies. It is the place where we learn to recognise Christ. The pain of the world, represented in that child's cry, must always encounter the beautiful music of the gospel. And the beautiful music of the gospel – this fourth movement we are called to play – must be sung and proclaimed within and for the sorrows of the world. Such is the priestly vocation: sharing in the priesthood of Christ and animating the priesthood of the whole people of God. Priests are called to tell the tale and sing the song of God's love. As the Ordination Prayer puts it: 'Give these your servants grace and power to proclaim the gospel of salvation and minister the sacraments of the new covenant …'[8]

And the prayer concludes: 'so shall a people made whole in Christ offer spiritual sacrifices acceptable to you our God and Father…'[9]

Here we have both the essence of the gospel *and* of ordained ministry; a ministry of word and sacrament for a people to be made whole in Christ and offer spiritual sacrifices to God. Ministry is always to the glory of God and for the building up of the people of God.

The weight of your calling

The Declaration made at ordination services finishes with an examination and ends with these awe-full words:

> In the name of our Lord we bid you remember the greatness of the trust that is now to be committed to your charge. Remember with thanksgiving that the treasure now to be entrusted to you is Christ's own flock, bought by the shedding of his blood on the cross. It is to him that you will render account for your stewardship of his people.[10]

This is a huge responsibility. The people of God, whom Christ brought into being by his death on the cross, is now committed to the care of the priest. One of the charisms of priestly ministry is that priests are stewards – stewards of the faith itself, stewards of the people of God, that is conductors in God's orchestra. If the second violin is out of tune or the percussion plays too loudly – as they often do in the orchestra of the church – and the melody, let alone the nuanced beauty of the harmony, is drowned out, we are responsible, we have to render account.

As I said earlier, these words – that it is Christ's own flock we care for and for which we will be asked to give an account – should make any sane person run screaming from the cathedral explaining that there has been a dreadful mistake, that the church has most certainly got the wrong person; and if anyone is mad enough to stay and be ordained then they are clearly so arrogant and deluded as to be unfit for the task anyway. But it is the Holy Spirit of Christ who calls and, as we have noted, the Declaration continues with these words of extraordinary comfort: 'You cannot bear the weight of this calling in your own strength, but only by the grace and power of God.'[11]

I will examine this in more detail in the next chapter. But for the moment, note the uncomfortable appearance of that word 'power' again. To be a priest is to be someone who is empowered with responsibility for the most precious things of the gospel itself – presiding at Holy Communion, declaring absolution, blessing God's people. That is why we receive this awesome responsibility with the servant heart of the deacon. Note also, the text with which I began this chapter: 'Think of us ... as servants of Christ and stewards of God's mysteries. Moreover, it is required of stewards that they should be found trustworthy' (1 Corinthians 4.1–2). 'Pray therefore, counsels the Ordinal, 'that your heart may daily be enlarged and your understanding of the scriptures enlightened. Pray for the gifts of the Holy Spirit.'[12]

This is what we need. As priests in the Church of God we need to be people whose hearts are enlarged, whose capacity for love is expanding. We must be servant *and* steward, deacon *and* priest. Our own intimate inhabiting of the gospel through prayer and study, and by a constant brooding over the Scriptures, mean that the people we serve and the gifts that they bring, ensure that the music of the gospel being played in our church is the same gospel of goodness and love that we heard in the earlier movements of the symphony.

In this way, our faithful stewardship ensures that the gospel lived and proclaimed in *one* church is the same gospel lived and proclaimed in *every* church. The church in Chelmsford or Charlton, in Chichester, Huddersfield, Hartlepool or Harlow is the same catholic Church as gathered in the upper room on the first Easter day and the same Church present in all places and in all times.

So, a question to end with, that all priests will need to ask themselves: Do you love the music?

Was it not the beautiful music of the gospel that first drew you to Christ and through Christ to exploring this particular vocation to serve as a priest in his Church? And where are you listening to the music today? How will you carry on listening to it tomorrow, so as to sustain yourself in all the tomorrows that lie ahead? What new rhythms and harmonies do you hear? And what variations will you play? How will you invite others to be part of it? These are the joys and challenges of priestly ministry.

And, yes, there are too many clergy who love the music, but think of themselves as a one-man – and it usually is 'man' in my experience – band. With a guitar over their shoulder, a bass drum strapped between their knees, tambourines on their ankles, a harmonica and a tin whistle, with castanets for earrings and a cymbal for a hat, they play the music themselves. As a result fewer and fewer people listen. Or else they think they *would* be stewards, but their church simply doesn't have sufficiently gifted people who could be trusted to minister themselves; or that the gospel is so precious as to be 'fragile' and needs protection from contamination by the world. Rowan Williams believes that God gives the Church all the gifts the Church needs to be the Church and he is right.

We must work with what God gives us, not what we desire. After all, isn't that what God is doing with us? The gospel may be precious, but it is also robust: it can quite easily take the knocks and bruises that come from being lived and shared generously.

So, finally, we must allow ourselves to be conducted. After all, we are stewarding the church on behalf of someone else. As Henri Nouwen has observed: 'If there is any hope for the Church in the future, it will be for a poor church in which its leaders are willing to be led.'[13]

Some scholars say that Bruckner never finished his ninth symphony because he couldn't. He just wasn't able to find the music to express the vision of glory that had seized him. It was inexpressible, beyond human conceiving; and therefore, they argue, it is fitting that it ends in a silence, an absence of conclusion. But surely this is – as it were – a fifth move-ment, the eighth day, the life of heaven, the great promise of the gospel to which we must always point, that life beyond this life, the sacraments themselves which we steward being mere signs and shadows of the presence of Christ himself in that city where there will be no temple nor sun but Christ himself as light and joy.

No, we are recruited as conductors in God's orchestra to love the music and to wield the baton, and to compose, with others, the life of the Church today which is the fourth move-ment in that great symphony of which God himself is the gracious composer who has enlisted us. This music is dedi-cated, as all Christian ministry must be, to *Leiber Menschheit* 'Dearest Humanity'.

So priests must love the people they serve. They are the ones for whom Christ died. They must teach the people they serve to play and love the music of the gospel. They must feed them with word and sacrament. They must make the words of the psalmist their own: 'O sing to the Lord a new song; sing his praise in the assembly of the faithful'; 'How good it is to make music to the Lord ...' (Psalms 149.1; 148.1).

Murmuration

there is a shared wind
of wingbeat
urging me to you
now
I find you
turning as like
to your own wing mate
who is like
turning to her own

we shape the air
   together
   falling
   as the breeze sweeps
   our common wing
rising as the heat
breast of the Earth
lifts us to the sky

MAX WOOLAVER
RECTOR OF ST ANDREW'S, GRIMSBY AND
ARCHDEACON OF LINCOLN IN THE DIOCESE OF NIAGARA

Part Three

CHAPTER SEVEN

Carrying the cross

If any want to become my followers, let them deny themselves and take up their cross and follow me.

MATTHEW 16.24

At a retreat during my curacy, the retreat conductor set us
the task of defining ministry. At the end of his address we
were sent off for an hour to reflect on our experience and
come up with a one-sentence definition. I can't remember
what we were supposed to do with the sentence: probably
something vaguely Celtic and cringingly relevant involving a
pebble, some water and lots of candles. Anyway, I stomped
off, not feeling terribly motivated about the task and genuinely
unsure about what to say. My experience of ministry at that
moment – I guess I had been ordained about two years – had
been a jumble of joys and horrors. There was only one thing
I was really sure of: my expensive training had not really
prepared me so well for the brutal facts of ministry. Indeed,
on a bad day it seemed like it had been carefully designed to
conceal me from reality. I knew a lot of New Testament
Greek. I could argue persuasively for my favoured position
of the epiclesis in post-Hippolytan Eucharistic Prayers. I even
had a passing knowledge of philosophy, theories of social

science, and the more advanced theories of group dynamics. But when I sat with the parents whose child had died and saw the utter bewildering helplessness in their eyes, I didn't have anything to say. And when the boy I had met in church on Sunday morning turned up at my house on Sunday evening and asked me whether I could give him twenty quid so that he could score some heroin, and if I didn't he would just have to go and rob someone, I was equally lost.

I'm not blaming my training. I enjoyed it enormously. And I also loved being a priest. But I found myself constantly convulsed by the greatest joys and the most heart-rending sorrows, and I never felt I had the resources within myself to deal with them. I wasn't either good enough, or holy enough or quick-witted enough. At the same time, the boundaries just kept shifting and the demands increasing.

There were also so many things that I realised I would only learn by my mistakes. Like the time the confirmation group just didn't want to talk to each other. Or to me. Or to anyone! Their boredom convicted me. Or in the school – easy to hype the children up, not so easy to get them to come down again. The raised eyebrows of the teachers into whose care I would return them after my fifteen minutes of frivolous havoc said it all.

At an even deeper level, the shaky foundations of my prayers were starting to show. At the sort of theological college I went to it was easy to think you were making progress in the spiritual life. After all, there were three services a day. Two of them were compulsory, and the other was attended by virtually everyone, so I went too. It seemed as if I was swimming. Actually, I was just being rushed along by the current. In the parish it was harder. Sometimes I was on my own. And in those moments of aloneness I found my spirituality was built on sand. Unsurprisingly, at the first signs of a crisis it collapsed. The call inside me was as strong as ever, the joys just about sufficient to carry me through the pain, but writing a definition? I simply couldn't think how ministry could be summed up, or tied down. All I knew was that I hadn't got it worked out. It was too complicated, too costly, too mysterious, and too beautiful. It wasn't the training that was the problem, it was me.

I wandered out of the building where we were meeting and headed down the road. It was drizzling. Around the corner was another church. The doors were open so I went in to shelter from the rain. I'm usually an optimistic sort of person, but I was discovering (and have now come to terms with) a need to face my own shadow. When I am alone, and particularly when I am on retreat, there is, for me, an encounter with darkness. This was one of my first.

Every priest carries an enormous burden of pain. We deal with things each day that are dark and difficult. We are familiar with unrepented sin and its terrible consequences in people's lives. But behind this encounter are other existential fears that test our own faithfulness and challenge our resolve. Why are we priests? Who are we trying to please? Is it all for nothing, and is our real motivation just a desperate attempt to convince ourselves that it is all true and worth it; that maybe if we really work hard at this God business (and if enough people say enough good things about us) we might even be properly converted ourselves (whatever that is)?

Anyway, I sat down in one of the pews and suddenly found myself feeling desperate and helpless. What was I doing? Who was I fooling? I felt the great tide of human suffering rushing towards me, and there was nothing I could do to stop it. Even the little successes of my ministry seemed inadequate.

Everything I was doing just seemed an act. I knew I wasn't the good and holy person some people supposed me to be. I also knew that for much of the time I was good at pretending to believe and say the right things, while my actual faith and my willingness to serve was very small indeed. Faced by real need and real suffering, and confronted with the truly hard questions of life and death, my spiritual resources were laughably poor. I was bound to be found out sooner or later. And, no, I couldn't define ministry: not in an essay, and certainly not in one sentence, and not even to myself. I felt useless. I was someone pretending to be a priest; someone who put on the clothes of a priest each morning, but whose inner life was as unconverted as anyone else's.

I think it was at this moment that I looked up. I was in an empty church, which itself suddenly seemed to be a symbol of how very fruitless my ministry was becoming. What I hadn't realised was that I was sitting beneath a picture of someone very like me. Just above me was the fifth Station of the Cross.

The Stations of the Cross are a series of images stationed at intervals around the walls of a church telling the story of the last hours of Jesus' earthly life, from his condemnation before Pilate to the placing of his body in the borrowed tomb. Introduced into the church by St Francis of Assisi, they gave the poor who would never be able to visit the Holy Land themselves the opportunity to enact in their own church a pilgrimage of hope, walking with Jesus to the cross and the grave and beyond. The fifth Station of the Cross depicts that small and strangely ambiguous episode in the story when the Roman guards get someone else to help the already flogged, exhausted and beaten Jesus carry his cross. In this church, beneath the picture of a kindly and benign helper lifting the cross of Christ to his own shoulders, an inscription read: Simon of Cyrene helps Jesus carry the cross.

Looking at the picture, remembering this little bit of the passion story, it suddenly seemed to me to be an answer to prayer – not that I was sure I *had* actually been praying, though perhaps a desolate and yearning heart is the best prayer of all. Reaching out to me from the passion of Christ itself there was an offering, at last an image I could hold onto and make sense of: a direct answer to the question that was rolling round my head. What was Christian ministry? Well, perhaps, it is just this. Perhaps this was all that I was being asked to do: to step from the crowd and bear the cross. It brought together my helplessness before the stranded passion of the bereaved parents and the confirmation class, the school assembly and the weekday Mass. In each situation I was called to bear the cross; or, to be more accurate, hold before the world the cross of Jesus Christ so that people could see it for themselves, and perhaps even glimpse in me, and in my actions and words, the saving power and the generous love of God.

It was such an obvious thought, but at the same time so liberating. My ministry was just one part of the whole ministry of all God's people; and what was that ministry except to bear Christ to the world, to witness to his death and resurrection? Nothing else was required of me except faithfulness to this vocation and then – as a priest in the Church – a singular dedication to enable more and more people to step out, to shoulder Christ's easy yoke of discipleship – for it is his ministry not ours – the releasing within the whole people of God of our vocation to be a priestly people. 'For when I am lifted up' promises Jesus, 'I will draw all people to myself'(John 12.32).

I suppose that was the day and that was the hour that I learned with my heart what I had been taught in my head: that ministry is not mine. That it belongs to God and it belongs to everyone. That it is God working through his Church, which is the body of Christ on earth. I would, in time, learn more and more about the particular tasks and responsibilities of ordained priesthood, but most of all I needed to see the personal dimensions of my own sharing in the ministry of Christ and the particular vocation to animate this ministry within everyone. I need to receive it as Christ's ministry in me, his accepting of my offer to help. All of it summed up in that moment, by the image of Simon stepping out of the crowd, helping Jesus bear the weight of the cross.

Inspired by this moment I then turned to look afresh at the scriptural accounts of this incident, and of course I was slightly thrown by what I found.

Mark describes it in this way: 'They *compelled* a passer-by, who was coming in from the country, to carry his cross' (Mark 15.21a). Matthew and Luke use the same language of pressure and compulsion. Luke even says that Simon is 'seized' (Luke 23.26).

This wasn't quite how the picture in the church conveyed it. This was not the image I had in my mind, where I was still the person in charge, willingly offering help, maintaining control. There was, therefore, one last thing I needed to learn and perhaps it is the most important thing of all.

All that I have said about personal allegiance to Christ and about the priest as the animator of the body is true, and of vital importance. We do that by focusing on the enabling of ministry, of releasing and equipping the whole people of God, and also by paying close attention to our own need of God and our own personal virtue and witness. But there is something else here in this story from Scripture that is uncomfortably relevant. Up until this point I had been thinking of Simon as a volunteer, and I had most certainly thought of myself as a volunteer. Now I realised he was a recruit. No, perhaps harder than that, a pressed man. He didn't want to carry that cross at all. He did it because he was compelled, because saying no wasn't an option. This was not about his generosity or heroism, but fear. He had no other choice. It says as much about his weakness as it does any strength he may possess.

Dare I look into those same dimensions of my own vocation? What other needs for popularity and power does my priesthood feed? What is my real motivation? Is it to willingly suffer alongside Christ, to bear his love to the world, to lead and feed his people? Or am I just trying to save myself? How honest am I about my own deep reluctance to know Christ, to do his will, and to follow in his way? And would I do anything at all, if I weren't pushed into it by the contours of the road I have ended up travelling?

The sober assessment of myself is this: I am both. I am volunteer *and* recruit; and utterly dependent on the Christ whose cross I so falteringly carry to purge me of the driven self-centeredness that slakes my own thirst only, and too easily ignores the suffering complexities of the world. Hardly a surprise really: this cross I carry, I need it just as much as everyone else. When I minister from this necessity, recognising my own need of God, realising I have nothing else to offer, and knowing that this gracious God can be alive in me, not to obliterate me but to fulfil me, so that in becoming the person I am meant to be – which includes for me being a priest in his Church – then I become the perfectly transparent vessel of his purposes, fully myself and completely Christ in me. I am a long way short of this. But God is good and gracious. All he looks for is my willingness to serve. Hence, ordained as a priest, I never stop being a deacon. And even as a bishop, still a servant for the servants. Some bishops wear a dalmatic – the deacon's distinctive vestment – underneath their chasuble as a reminder.

Of course Jesus models this ministry for us perfectly. As the Introduction to the ordination liturgy puts it: 'Priests are to set the example of the Good Shepherd always before them as the pattern of their calling.'[1] It is Jesus' own example of joyful and obedient waiting upon God that sustains and motivates us. Jesus only does what he sees the Father doing, and so, in turn, priests, and for that matter all God's people, should only do what they see in Christ. Volunteer or recruit, Jesus accepts Simon's help, and so he accepts us with all our confusions and unworthiness. No, more than that: he is the one who has called us and compelled us out of the crowd, because if there was no confusion, if there was no unworthiness, there would be no cross. We are here because he wants us to be here, and because we can be used, and in being used we can be fulfilled in his ministry of generous self-giving.

This is the essence and the joy of priestly ministry. It is renewed and sustained at the Lord's Table, when with bread and wine we hold up his passion, death and resurrection for all to see and all to receive. It is this – and only this – that priests must do: bear the cross of Christ. Encourage others to do the same. Show it to the world, for Jesus tells his disciples that if we are to be his followers then we must carry the cross, and that if we don't do this we are not his followers at all (see Luke 14.27).

We must show the world that this way of the cross is, indeed, the path to life; that it is in losing our lives for his sake that we truly find them (see Matthew 16.25). There is a warning as well however: 'What will it profit them if they gain the whole world but forfeit their life?' (Matthew 16.26).

These are particularly sobering words for a priest. All Christians are easily tempted to strut the wider road approved of by the world, rather than the narrow way required by Christ. But when a priest walks this way, not only do they lose their own soul, but in squandering their ministry, risk losing others.

One last thing: in his account of the story, Mark adds the intriguing detail that Simon of Cyrene is 'the father of Alexander and Rufus' (Mark 15.21b) as if those hearing the account would know immediately who was being spoken about – as if to say, you know, so and so's Dad.

Just as interestingly, and in a way confirming the point, Matthew and Luke omit this detail. Their audiences won't know who he's talking about. Simon of Cyrene has now become a 'name', not a person anyone is directly attached to. He is remembered only as the one the soldiers seized from the crowd and was made to help Jesus.

How will we be remembered? For the time being, and I hope that all priests, throughout their ministries, will be known by the people they serve, and others who will come to know Christ through them. They will say, even when they are speaking of Christ, that it was through this priest's witness that Christ was known. They might even associate the church where they serve with them, because it will be their leadership and their example that drew them to Christ and caused the flourishing of ministry in that place. All this will pass though. Every priest and every bishop is just the latest in a long line of those to whom the baton of the gospel is passed. It is of this gospel that we are servants.

Look at the list of incumbents in a country church, sometimes dating back centuries. Be inspired by that faithful witness. We do not know who they were, yet their names are honoured and remembered and, most important of all, known to God. Through them the Church flourished. May it also flourish through those God is calling into ordained ministry today. All that is required is the same faithfulness: whether we feel like it or not; on the days when we are a willing volunteer, and also on the days when we are a pressed recruit. We offer it all to Christ as best we can, and let him and his Holy Spirit do the rest. For God will be at work in us. He will use the gifts and time and experience we offer, and in bearing the cross of Christ we will be servants of the gospel, priests in the Church of Jesus Christ.

CHAPTER EIGHT

Guarding the heart

Keep your heart with all vigilance,
for from it flow the springs of life

PROVERBS 4.23

Writing to the troubled and troublesome church in Corinth Paul said that he did not come 'proclaiming the mystery of God to you in lofty words or wisdom. For I decided to know nothing ... except Jesus Christ, and him crucified.' He admits that he came in 'in weakness and in fear and in much trembling' (see 1 Corinthians 2.1−3). Now this is an appropriate text for the night before an ordination and I have preached on it at ordination charges to those whom I have ordained on several occasions: I come with nothing to offer but Jesus Christ. And I come in weakness, fear and trembling.

However ill equipped people feel for the task of proclaiming the gospel, I am always fairly confident that they are all very well qualified in the weakness, fear and trembling department. During Evening Prayer before I speak to them I am sure I hear knees knocking.

Make no mistake about it, both are necessary. I don't want to ordain anyone who thinks they have a gospel of their own to deliver. And I don't want to ordain anyone who is not fearful and awestruck and very conscious of their own weaknesses and their lack of readiness or ability. We come with the gospel of Jesus Christ, and we dress it up in nothing but the simple truths and daunting challenges of the Scriptures; we preach, commend and explain it through the lens of our own life of discipleship, the hope that is within us, knowing that this gospel is saving truth for our own lives as much as anyone else's. Every sermon that every minister preaches must first be preached to themselves. And if it doesn't address the cancer in our own soul, and if it doesn't convert us, and if it doesn't challenge us to rise up and follow in the path of discipleship, then it won't heal, convert or challenge anyone else.

It is perfectly normal for anyone being ordained to feel anxious about their readiness or ability, especially on the night before their ordination. It is also why it is my happy duty to remind them why they are there and also reprimand them if, by overstating their unworthiness, they actually end up claiming to know better than God.

Of course those who are ordained are unworthy! Of course they are not up to it. Who is! But none of that is the point. As the centurion famously said to Jesus, demonstrating a faith that Jesus had not witnessed much before – words that we echo in the response we make each time we receive Holy Communion – we are not worthy: but you say the word and we are healed (see Matthew 8.5–13).

This is why we must guard our hearts, remembering that we are unworthy; but not letting that unworthiness derail our ministry. Isn't this why we take Holy Communion? As Rowan Williams has put it, 'not because we are doing well, but because we are doing badly. Not because we have arrived, but because we are travelling. Not because we are right, but because we are confused and wrong. Not because we are divine, but because we are human. Not because we are full, but because we are hungry.'[1]

Find enough time to sleep, enough time to pray,
then do what you can

When I was ordained deacon, my ordination retreat was led by the somewhat eccentric and deeply holy priest, the one-time Principal of St Stephen's House, Fr Derek Allen. I must have been going through a holy phase, because I kept a retreat notebook, and as well as a few rather obvious observations of my own, I jotted down some of things he said during the retreat. A few years ago I came across this journal, and was interested to thumb through it and encounter what I was thinking and feeling at that point of embarkation to ordained ministry. Derek Allen concluded his final retreat address with the words: 'Find enough time to sleep, find enough time to pray, and then do what you can.' I think I might have written this down because at the time it seemed absurd. Was this the best advice he could offer at such a moment, this seemingly innocuous charge to sleep and pray and then get on with it?

Now, many years later, I see the wisdom of what he was saying.[2] Ordained ministry in God's Church is now your life, and this life must be built on two priorities more than any other — time for yourself and time for God.

First of all, then, what does it mean to give time to God?

A few years ago I was chatting with someone about to be ordained, asking them what they had valued most in their preparation for ordination. They had trained at a residential theological college and had found that the disciplined life of daily prayer had been the thing that had made the biggest impact. It had anchored them in something larger than themselves and sustained them in everything that followed. However, they then went on to lament that all this would have to change when they got into the parish!

I responded by asking why they thought they were being ordained. Actually, my language was rather stronger! I said, 'What the bloody hell do you think you are being ordained for?' Was it to a life of feverish activity, or was it to a life of prayer? And, anyway, with all the competing demands of all the things they *could* be doing, wouldn't such an anchor and such a means of sustenance not only continue to sustain them in their ordained ministry, but also help shape the choices and the decisions they made about the best use of the limited time and resources they – like everyone – had to offer?

Of course, as ordained ministers, we do things. Of course, there is an awful lot to do! But let us not delude ourselves. The things that you actually have to do to as a priest are not so many. Once you have led the services on Sunday, chaired the PCC, and buried the dead, there is not such a huge list of stuff that absolutely has to be done. What you *could* do is limitless and neverending. One of the hardest home truths for clergy to face is that when we are too busy and our diary too full, it is not because of all the things we *had* to do, but the things we *chose* to do. Indeed, the greatest and most practical wisdom that every priest must acquire in order for their ministry to be fruitful is the gift of discernment about what to do – what to pick up, and what to put down, and how to lead and build a church where ministry is the work of everyone. Many clergy never achieve this. They often end up washed out or burned up. It is a desperately sad sight.

They will also complain: about the congregation, with whom they would share ministry if they weren't such a dull bunch; about the diocese – all its red tape and bureaucracy are really to blame. But never themselves.

This is essentially a spiritual issue. It is about seeking a life that is lived in community with God. The important question is this: Is the love of God and the love of the gospel the motivation behind all that I do? And is prayer and the nurturing of the spiritual life the wellspring of my ministry?

The life of prayer, and nurturing the life of prayer, is the heart of ministry. It will express itself in many different ways. Just as we have different personalities, and have been shaped by different traditions of the Church, so we will pray in different ways. There will be some constants, however, that we must pay attention to. First of all, the disciplines of the Daily Office. The daily readings of psalm and Scripture, and some silent pondering of the word of God, is essential for the priestly life. It saves prayer from being about how I am feeling at any one time. It unites my prayer with the prayer of the whole Church worldwide. And even if I'm not actually using the formal prayer book of my church (though, unsurprisingly, this is what I would recommend), a disciplined pattern of prayer that I enter into because I know it is right and good and will serve me in the long term far better than any reliance on my own resources or mood.

Many priests discover that presiding at the Eucharist becomes a bedrock and a lifeline for their own spirituality. This has definitely been my experience.

Time away – a regular quiet day or an annual retreat – is vital, as is some sort of spiritual guidance, be it through a spiritual director, a soul friend or a cell group. It is easier to delude yourself in the spiritual life than in almost any other walk of life, so some accountability to a trusted other is the best way of holding yourself to account for the promise all priests make to 'be diligent in prayer'.[3]

This spiritual nurture differs little whether you are a stipendiary or a self-supporting minister. For those who receive a stipend, ministry is funded by the gifts and generosity of others. But it is a stipend, not a wage, so that you *don't* have to go out to work! There is no contract. There is no tallying up the hours at the end of the month. No clocking on and clocking off. You are given a house and a stipend to be free of all this. What a tragedy it would be if such a gift was squandered by just being busy all the time, and anxiously fretting about how many hours 'you've worked'. Rather, the gift must be used to pray; to grow in faith; to discern the best ways of leading the church and using time. If it is just another job, where you feverishly count hours and tick off tasks, you will either go mad, go AWOL, or be burnt out or washed up in a few years' time.

For those who are self-supporting ministers and worker priests, time is actually no more or less limited than those who are stipendiary. It may be the case that these clergy offer fewer hours on the mechanics of the Church institution than their stipendiary colleagues, but all ordained ministry is about the whole of life. You don't become a priest at nine and clock off at five. Ministry can't just be something that is put on when you leave work and do something specifically ministerial. Priesthood is the response of the whole life to the call of God. If I learn to think of it as a life offered to God in the service of the gospel, and if I am first of all a person of prayer, a minister of word and sacrament, someone who broods upon the Scriptures and waits patiently on God, then I will be relaxed and fulfilled in this ministry. I will fully be a priest all the time, even if – such as when I sleep, or when I am going about that part of my working life that is not obviously priestly – my priesthood is hidden. We must stop using the language of 'full time' and 'part time'. It is all nonsense. We are all limited in the time we have to offer. What we need to do is make the best use of the time that is available, and the best way of doing this is to establish a proper discipline about giving time to God, making it the first foundation of ministry and taking advantage of the rhythms and pattern of ministry. So in August, when the load tends to be lighter, we don't feel guilty about taking some additional time off. And in December or in Lent when there are many evening commitments and so many more opportunities to serve and witness, we enter it joyfully, not counting hours or feeling hard done by.

Which leads to the second, equally vital, priority that Derek Allen identified all those years ago: keep the Sabbath day holy! This is surely what he meant by saying, "find enough time to sleep', though I want to put it this way: make sure you take a day off each week.

In the Bible the Sabbath is both a gift of God in creation, and a commandment. Sometimes I think it only became a commandment because we failed to receive it as a gift. We saw it as the fag end of the creation, an exhausted God taking to his bed after the enormous labour of making a universe, rather than the climax of the creation where God rests in and enjoys the good creation God has made. Sabbath, and the principle of Sabbath that there should be order and balance to life, is vital for healthy living. In a frantic and driven society like ours, it should be one of the main ways we demonstrate an alternative way of inhabiting the world, where we appreciate and cherish the creation and its natural rhythms and balance. We are not biblical fundamentalists, so for clergy, the Sabbath can't be Sunday. We should all make sure, however, that there is at least one day each week that we give to rest, recreation and reflection. Thus we establish a biblical pattern for living.

In the world of work there is usually a ring fence around the hours of work. There is a contract telling you your hours, and if you go over it you may get paid overtime, but even if you don't, or if you take work home, you are aware that a boundary has been crossed.

In the biblical pattern of living, and in the pattern I am suggesting is foundational for fruitful priestly ministry, the boundary is the other way round. The Sabbath is a commandment, so we ring fence our leisure. We identify one day where rest and recreation and time for family and friends and the nurturing of good relationships is the priority. It is not that everything outside of this day is 'work', and we burn ourselves out working stupidly long hours. Everything else is our *life* as a priest in God's Church. If this life is built on these twin foundations – time for God and time for Sabbath – Derek Allen's words will come true: the 'do what you can' will be not only significant but also fruitful. It will be balanced, focused and sustainable too. It will be a partnership with God and a partnership with others. It will be the overflow of that intimacy with God and with yourself and your family that is a well-ordered life of rest and prayer. As Jesus warned, using the image of ministry and ministers as vines and branches: 'apart from me you can do nothing' (John 15.5).

Of course we all often get this wrong; and I say this here, not because I have such a worked-out spirituality, but because

I have fallen many times and have learned the hard way that ministry is most fruitful when I am attending to my roots rather than artificially trying to force feed the fruit.

It is also the case, and we see this again and again in the rhythms and patterns of Jesus' own ministry, that it is from these reservoirs of watching and waiting upon God that good decisions and appropriate strategies emerge. It is only after prayer that Jesus is able to say no to the demands of people in one place and go and preach the gospel in another (see Mark 1.35–9). It is only after prayer, and real pleading with God that there might be another way, that Jesus is able to receive the cup the Father gives and drain it to the dregs (see Mark 14.32–42).[4]

We, too, in the course of ministry, face competing demands, the projections and expectations of many good people (and quite a few loveably dodgy ones as well!). We are faced with excruciatingly hard decisions. We need to take many risks. Sometimes we are asked to do things that we don't want to do, and go to places where we don't want to go, whether it be a parish that isn't quite our tradition – though let's be honest, does God really care one jot for the traditions of the Church? – or a pastoral visit to a bereaved family whose child has died, or to speak about the gospel to a hostile audience.

It is also the disciplines of rest and prayer that will enable us to keep ourselves in perspective, remembering the things we are called to do, but most of all helping us remember this ministry we share is God's not ours. It is entrusted to the whole Church of which we are servant, shepherd, messenger, sentinel and steward.

I think this is what is meant by the proverb with which I began this chapter: guard your heart. We should pay attention to the things that are the source and wellsprings of ministry and life. Seek first the kingdom of God, then everything else will be given to you (see Matthew 6.33). In this way, ministry will be fruitful because it is God's ministry in us, and we will be able to give and go on giving from the overflow of what we are receiving. Our re-creation and replenishment as people of rest and prayer are the keys to a ministry which will use our gifts in the service of the gospel and also in the service of the Church whose priestly people we are called to lead. Therefore, we must be as a tree planted by living water, bearing fruit in good season (See Psalm 1.3)

It will also mean that we must all minister from a place of need, constantly aware that it is not our ministry but God's, and that we are not doing it because of our worthiness or holiness, but because God has called us and that this vocation is a part of the divine mystery as it is lived out in us, part of our own self actualisation and salvation. This too may have to be learned the hard way, but priesthood is always about our own salvation as much as sharing God's salvation with others.

I'm reminded of a wonderful story that Rowan Williams tells, about a distinguished senior bishop of the Church of England who had been brought up in a very strict Protestant sect. As a teenager he began to study the Bible seriously, and when he read 1 Corinthians, he was surprised to discover that the Church of the Bible was apparently full of greedy, lecherous, drunken, disreputable characters, who needed the stern words of St Paul to bring them into line. Then, having recognised the nature of the biblical Church, he duly decided to join the Church of England. 'Not a completely serious defence of the C of E, perhaps. But it underlines the point that what matters about the Church is less our achievement than God's gift. It is when we look at the gift that we see what it means to think of the Church as heaven on earth, a human group caught up into the action of God.'[5]

It is probably at the Eucharist that we grasp this biblical truth most explicitly and why many Christians speak of the Church's worship, especially Holy Communion, as 'heaven on earth'. Eastern Orthodox Christians typically insist that the worship of the Church is the presence of heaven on earth; and in doing so they are entirely in tune with what St Paul wants to say about the Church's life as a whole.

Rowan Williams simply describes this as living as those who 'know that they are always guests – that they have been welcomed and that they are wanted ... In Holy Communion Jesus Christ tells us that he wants our company.'[6] It also means recognising that my neighbour, however irritating and repellent I find them, is also wanted by God.

It is the sacred duty of a priest to be the presider, the overseer, at this celebration, uniting the Church in this time with the Church in every time, representing Christ to his people and feeding them with the bread of heaven. But it is also the priest's own salvation that as a fellow sinner, as much in need of God's grace as anyone else, they come to this table with empty hands and ask, and ask again, that the Lord may forgive them their sins, fill them with his grace, and replenish them for God's service in the world.

It is a great joy to be a priest. Most of us find that it is as we preside at the Eucharist that our vocation and our role within the body at last seems to make real sense. I long for the priests I serve to be filled with the joy of the gospel, to guard their hearts, and to keep returning to the wells of salvation that the Lord Jesus Christ has dug in the barren earth of human frailty and failure; for now the desert is blossoming, the wood of the cross bursts into life, in the Valley of Achor doors of hope are opened, and God calls men and women to priestly ministry within the priestly people of God.

Other authorised and licensed ministries

Let's consider for a moment the duty of a priest to guard, cherish and encourage the other ministries that build up the Church and serve the kingdom. Because ministry is collaborative we should expect each church to have people in it who can share in the pastoral care, the leading of worship, the proclaiming of the gospel and the teaching of the Christian faith. They will do this through volunteer ministries such as teaching in the Sunday School and leading the intercessions; others will receive training and authorisation as lay preachers, pioneer ministers and evangelists. Some will be selected and trained as Readers or Licensed Lay Ministers. Some will be called to ordination. Everyone has a ministry, which is their share in the apostolic ministry of Christ and is lived out day to day in their home, their community and their place of work. All will have some sort of part to play in the life of the local church, and some of the most domestic ministries —of making the coffee, mowing the grass in the churchyard, or lighting up the boiler on a winter's morning – will be the most valuable, because they are the ministry of service, often, hidden ministries that facilitate the ministry of the whole church. All must be encouraged and valued. But where we find people with particular gifts and callings to particular ministries, there is a special responsibility to encourage them so that the whole church works together for the whole world, and that everyone is equipped and encouraged to be ambassadors of Christ in their daily life.

These are also the people who under our care are to be kept in the way of salvation and nurtured in the Christian faith. This is a special responsibility.

As already quoted, the Ordinal sums up the immensity of this rather well:

> Remember always with thanksgiving that the treasure now to be entrusted to you is Christ's own flock, bought by the shedding of his blood on the cross. It is to him that you will render account for your stewardship of his people.[7]

It also counsels that as we cannot bear the weight of this calling in our own strength we must pray that our hearts may daily be enlarged.[8] Which I suppose means: Remember why you're here and whose ministry it is. It means following Jesus.

Leading like Jesus

Just as we are called to follow Jesus, a priest is also required to lead like Jesus. Leading like Jesus means expanding our capacity for compassion, empathy, concern for justice, and love. We do this by emptying ourselves of all that is not of God – our self-referential and self-preoccupied ways of inhabiting the world and the ways we screen ourselves from God. It is worth emphasising that religion – and a lot of it – is one of the very best ways of avoiding God. It is a constant spiritual danger for a priest; we spend so much time in church talking *to* God and *about* God, reckoning ourselves experts *on* God, that we find it all too easy to avoid listening to what God might actually be saying.

Leading like Jesus often means leading in ways that the world will find either naive or objectionable. Currently, there is a huge leadership industry. Leadership consultants get paid big money to advise you on vision, strategy and its implementation. Although there is much we can learn from the successes of the world, in the Church we will also try to remember the warnings of Jesus, particularly wrestling with what he says to the disciples when they boil over with righteous anger because James and John's mother has asked for special places for her sons in the kingdom of God. First of all, Jesus replies they are not on offer. James and John may be able to drink the cup that Jesus drinks (that is, share in his suffering), but places on his left and right will go to the criminals who are crucified alongside him (see Matthew 20.20–3). Then to the ten he says:

> You know that the rulers of the Gentiles lord it over them, and their great ones are tyrants over them. It will not be so among you; but whoever wishes to be great among you must be your servant, and whoever wishes to be first among you must be your slave; just as the Son of Man came not to be served but to serve, and to give his life a ransom for many.
>
> MATTHEW 20.24–8

Asserting that 'It will not be so among you' is Jesus deliberately turning his back on the leadership models of the world. This is why: as I mentioned right at the beginning of the book – and to the surprise of many clergy – the word 'leader' doesn't appear as such in the New Testament or in the Christian tradition. This doesn't mean not leading at all. It means leading differently; letting the words of the Ordinal we have explored in this book shape the leaders we are called to be. As Nicholas Henshall has movingly put it:

> Christians have found it extremely easy to forget all this. Words for the consecration of the ministry of ordained elders swiftly shifted ground from the simple, fairly colour-less New Testament word 'laying on of hands' (*cheirotonesis*) to the secular Latin word *ordinatio*, the word for installing a magistrate. Gradually different grades of ordained elders adopted splendidly hierarchical robes – power dressing with a range of elaborate headgear, despite Jesus' absolute clarity about the need for the church to subvert precisely such power. Every time I put on the traditional vestments for the Eucharist I am profoundly conscious that these are not the distinctive robes of a Christian priest, but the borrowed robes of a fourth century Roman official. That does not necessarily mean they should not be worn. Rather that the wearer and the worshipping community should understand the irony.[9]

We have to conclude, then, that we too must not be beguiled or seduced by models of leadership that promise success but turn their back on servanthood. 'It will not be so among you' says Jesus. On the contrary, we must always make sure there is room in our hearts for those things we see in him: compassion, empathy, mercy, concern for justice and love. Or as Jesus himself puts it in the Beatitudes: 'Blessed are the poor in spirit, for theirs is the kingdom of heaven' (Matthew 5.3). Which I think means, 'Blessed are those who do not take themselves too seriously. Blessed are those who are not self-sufficient. Blessed are those who are prepared to look for resources outside themselves. Blessed are those who are not full of their own ideas, but who wait patiently upon God. Blessed are those who are ready to be filled and who are therefore prepared to be empty.' Or as it is sometimes put: 'Blessed are those who know their need of God.'

This beatitude leads to all the others. It is the doorway into that set of attitudes which shape and define the Christian life, where we learn meekness and purity of heart, to lament and to be merciful, to hunger and thirst for what is right, and to make peace as children of God's kingdom, recognising all the time that to follow Jesus will mean persecution – be it apathy, ridicule or violence itself.

Let's not make the mistake of thinking persecution only happens to Christians in other parts of the world. The way of life we offer in Christ is profoundly opposed to so much of what passes for normal in our world today. Our call to love neighbour and to live as a global community will bring us into conflict with others who want the world smaller, and just for themselves.

However, as we have seen, the Ordinal goes on: 'Pray that your heart may daily be enlarged, *and your understanding of the Scriptures enlightened. Pray earnestly for the gift of the Holy Spirit.*'[10] Pray for nothing else then. Your heart enlarged. Your understanding of Scriptures enlightened. The Holy Spirit to guide and comfort you in all that lies ahead.

More than anything else, we must be a Church that loves. Love is itself the medicine of the gospel, and the summing up of all that God is, and all that God is doing in Christ. There is no more sorry a sight in the Church than a priest who does not love the people they serve. If we fail to love, then we are failing the gospel itself. In the words of St

Ambrose, 'First and foremost, we need to realise that there is nothing more helpful than to be loved and nothing more hurtful or devoid of benefit than not being loved.'[11]

Without the giving and receiving of this love all our efforts will be worth nothing.. If you doubt it, read again that great thirteenth chapter of Paul's first letter to the church in Corinth. Remember, the context in which he writes is ministry in the Spirit.

The Holy Spirit is the great minister in the Church. The Holy Spirit will inspire and sustain us and make up what is lacking. Therefore, we must pray earnestly for the gifts of the Spirit, not just today but every day, and in all that lies ahead in a lifetime of ministry, however it is that God is calling you to serve. God has great plans for each of us. In ministry we go to places and do things that cannot be imagined and that cannot be secured in our own strength or from the limits of our own imagination and resources. But with the Holy Spirit all things are possible. Just as the Holy Spirit came upon Mary, so that Jesus was born in her, so God can be alive in us and through our ministry if we pray each day for the gifts of the Spirit, and especially the gift of love.

This book is written in the hope of inspiring and informing a next generation of leaders in God's Church: leaders filled by the Holy Spirit and overflowing with love the world needs; ministers of word and sacrament, servants, shepherds, messengers, sentinels and stewards of the Lord; people who love and are open to being loved, and who will go on loving; people who serve and are open to being served, and who will go on serving.

It will be around God's table at the Eucharist that anyone who is called to the priesthood will find themselves most keenly aware of the immensity of this calling and of God's great confidence in them, but also that it is not really their ministry at all. It is God the Holy Spirit at work in his Church.

Saying the words that Jesus said, and acting in his name, a priest is both the one who represents Christ to the people and the one who brings the people to Christ. This is the priestly vocation. We must wear it well.

Why are you weeping?

The odds are that it's Monday
the usual clergy day off –
I guess it makes me a second day Adventist.
It's the day I let my guard down
and it's a day that I often go to a movie
and did I mention that I'm Irish?
Now that's a dangerous combination and
my eyes fill like the backyard rain barrel after
an Easter shower.

> But this only answers the 'why' of the condition –
> not the 'why' of the reason.

Perhaps it's the pause of sabbath in the midst of
feelings of relentless responsibilities
and the infinite 'coulds' and 'shoulds'.

Perhaps it's an opportunity for inconvenient emotions
needfully and professionally kept under control during
counselling; palliative bedside; funeral or
the revelation of terrible diagnosis –
    to let loose –
in the safety of a darkened tomb-like movie theatre.

Perhaps it's the glimpse of my own mortality
revealed in the mortality of others and my own
aches and pains.

But perhaps, just perhaps, it is the beauty of one
whose costly love includes even
me, whose light
a pillar in the blackness gives
unkillable life
and who bottles up
these tears, calling me
by name

JAMES ROBINSON
RECTOR OF ST AUGUSTINE'S, LETHBRIDGE, IN THE
DIOCESE OF CALGARY

Being found

You know those dreams where you find yourself in front of a crowd in nothing but your underwear? I have them too, but they're of an ecclesiastical flavour. They're always about me discovering that the only available cope is of some dreadful modern design, or in finding that my cassock has been eaten by moths, or even arriving at Mass having left my surplice in the laundry room at home.

Isn't it queer that the wearing of vestments should be the subject of my dreams?

Vestments, we're told, are meant to erase the personality of the priest so that the congregation will concentrate on the rite and not the celebrant. That may be so, but I'm sure I dream of them because they make me feel safe, because it's so easy to hide behind all of those silken protections and in the persona of 'The Dean'. And I wonder if the reason I fit so easily and immediately into that role is because I really don't want to be known for who I am, because I am trying to hide my deepest self, because being grandly pompous is so much safer than being authentically vulnerable. Except Christ's power and appeal lies in the fact that he was unafraid to be who he was and thought it no shame to be stripped naked and lifted high for all the world to see. So I dream of the day when I'll be courageous enough to dance a spiritual dance of the seven veils, drop all pretences and pretentions and stand emotionally naked before the Church. It won't be pleasant and it sure won't be pretty. But it will be real. And at least I'll be ready to truly put on Christ and finally learn that for those who do so there is no shame but rather the glorious liberty found in being

found in him and in being given the greater dignity of the
meek king.

LEIGHTON LEE
DEAN OF CALGARY

AFTERWORD

The ministry of a bishop

Sermon preached at the consecration of John Wraw and Tim Dakin, St Paul's Cathedral, 25 January 2012 – the Feast of the Conversion of St Paul.

The Lord said to Ananias as he set off on his unenviable task:

> Go, for he [Paul] is an instrument whom I have chosen to bring my name before gentiles and kings and before the people of Israel; I myself will show him how much he must suffer for the sake of my name.

ACTS 9.15B, 16

In Canto 18 of the second part of Dante's *Divine Comedy*, by the time Virgil completes his discourse on love and free will, the moon is high in the sky. Dante is just dozing off when he is, and I quote, 'roused by the noisy approach of the slothful!'[1]

This is how it works in Purgatory. It is 'where human spirits purge themselves, and train to leap up into joy celestial'.[2] There are seven terraces, each of which corresponds to one of the seven capital sins. And in purgatory the punishment – or should we say the means of purification – fits the crime.

Thus it is that Dante is roused by the slothful. Clad in lycra, wiping perspiration from their brow, and with an everlasting subscription to the gym, their penance is to jog. Likewise we may suppose that the lustful are locked in a room watching party political broadcasts from the 1970s and the test card on an endless loop; the wrathful spend their days being 'listened to'; the envious look in a mirror; and the gluttonous are signed up to Weight Watchers, nibbling an eternity's supply of rice cakes and bran.

Well, I don't know about purgatory, but there is some wisdom here. God gets us in the end. He works on our shadow. He is inside out. And you can tell the offence by observing the penalty. So why, on the road to Damascus, would God seize the vision of a man like Saul? Well, it is blindingly obvious: Saul saw things too clearly. Here was a man with a sure touch, a clear head, a strategic mind – episcopal material if ever I saw it. And yet it was not enough. Not only was it not enough, it had become the very enemy of all God's purposes, bent on destroying the infant Church with the awful, bloody clarity of the misdirected single mind. To bring this mind to a place of refining darkness an even greater light was required. One that reduces before it expands. One that darkens before it brings to light.

Sometimes it feels to me that ministry – all ministry, but maybe especially episcopal ministry – is like running up the down escalator. It can be done. And if, like me, you remember doing it as a boy, you will know that it carries with it a certain triumphant exhilaration. It certainly requires a singleness of mind and a very determined best foot forward. But what you mustn't ever do is stop. The trouble is as life goes on, and the escalators seem longer and faster, the only option is to run faster and longer yourself.

Brothers and sisters, I have a dream. I have a dream of a different way of doing ministry. I have a dream of an up escalator. I believe there is a way of doing what we must do, and achieving what we must achieve, but in a way that is less dependent on us and on our hard work. And I believe that in order to find it we may have to stop running. We may have to let God lead us to a place of darkness, blindness, unknowing. And there, in the utter lostness of that place, he will turn us around and show us his way. That's what is happening on those seven terraces that Dante spoke about. It is what God is doing to Saul on the road to Damascus: giving him a new name and a new identity, making him Paul.

John. Tim. It is what God wants to do in you. He wants to bring you again to a place of refining, where you will learn to trust him. And we bishops need this more than most, because, as you will quickly discover, it is a beguiling and seductive role. People treat us — and they mean it well — as if we are something special. When you arrive at a church a parking space will be ready for you. Someone will be waiting to greet you and to carry your bag. Someone will be on hand should you need to pass them your staff or take off your mitre. You will have PAs, secretaries, chaplains, drivers, advisers, gardeners, caterers. You will not have to make phone calls. Someone will put you through. You will not open your own post. You will not fill in your own diary. You will learn not to think out loud (that would be policy!). You will talk a lot. And I mean an awful lot. Talk after talk after sermon after sermon. The sound of your own voice, chattering on about every subject under the sun will become the soundtrack of your life. You will be an important person. People will say all sorts of things about you – usually behind your back. But in public and for most of the time, they will believe your publicity, and you will doubtless come to do the same. And then one day, when someone forgets to put the cones out for your car, and no one is there to carry your bag, or you are not asked to say a few words, you will fume with simmering resentment.

John. Tim. We need to be a different sort of bishop. Missionary and pilgrim rather than Master or Lord. Why? Because there is only one Master and Lord and we serve him.

O God, give the church leaders who know how to be led, and then following in Christ's footsteps, we will find our way to joy.

'Saul, Saul, why are you persecuting me?' This is what God said to Paul on the Damascus Road. And, finally, isn't this what Paul had to learn more than anything else in the darkness of his refining 'visionless vision'? And isn't this what we bishops need to learn too? The Church belongs to God. It is his, not ours. No, more than this, it is not God's possession, it is the body on earth of his beloved son Jesus Christ into which we are incorporated. We bishops are not local branch managers of Church of England plc; we are those limbs and organs of Christ's body who are charged with specific responsibility to pastor and evangelise. It is our role to encourage and equip the Church for ministry, 'fostering the gifts of the Spirit in all who follow Christ'[3] and then telling – above all, telling – the story of God's love in Christ, witnessing to all that he has done in our own lives, 'proclaiming the gospel boldly, confronting injustice and working for righteousness and peace in the world'.[4] John and Tim, confound the people of Basildon and Basingstoke, of Romsey and Rayleigh with the truth and beauty of Christ (see Acts 9.22).

I remember recently doing that thing I'm sure we all do in schools where children grill the bishop in the classroom for a few minutes. The questions are quite predictable: Bishop, how much do you earn? More than a paper boy and less than the Prime Minister. Which football team do you support? The mighty Spurs. And then coming in under the radar, rocking me for a moment: Bishop what do you actually do? And I replied: I am a voice. I am a pair of hands. And now I want to add that, yes, there have been, and will be, moments of wretchedness and darkness, when I don't know what I'm doing and I don't know what to say, and in these moments, like in the gospel itself, where the sky blackens as Jesus hangs upon the cross, and where God raises him in the darkness before the dawn, it is in the refining emptiness that I learn to trust God and become again his voice and his hands to do his will and purpose for the world. John. Tim. This is what God asks of you. For his people in Essex and East London, in Hampshire, East Dorset, the Channel Islands – these places and people that he loves. Be his hands and voice. Let him take all the rich experiences of your lives and ministry; all the things that have led you to be called and chosen for this high office, and let him cleanse and refine you. Be 'an instrument in God's hands' so that Christ may be known. Let him lead you into the darkness as well as into light.

ACKNOWLEDGEMENTS

I suppose any book about priesthood must acknowledge those who taught and formed the author in their own priestly ministry. For me, that means turning to the priests who inspired me: Fr Stroud, Vicar of St Margaret's, Leigh-on-Sea, where I learned and received the Christian faith, and a succession of curates – David Broome, Paul James and Richard Buckingham in particular. I trained for ordination at St Stephen's House in Oxford. David Hope was Principal at the time, and he was the main reason that I went there. He showed me what a prayerful priestly life looks like. But I also learned much from fellow ordinands, not least my friend Martin Warner who is now, like me, a bishop in the Church of England, and also from those priests with whom I have been in a cell group for the past thirty-six years.

I served my title in the Southwark Diocese at Christ Church and St Paul's, Forest Hill. My training incumbent, John Caldecott, was hugely patient with me. He was the one who taught me how to preside at the Eucharist (the weekly Mass classes began after Christmas for my ordination at Petertide, so I was extremely well prepared).

Over the years many other clergy, particularly from Evangelical traditions in the Church, have helped me understand ministry in new and complementary ways. I'm particularly mindful of the things I learned from colleagues such as Steven Croft, Robert Warren, James Lawrence, Martin

Cavender, Angela Butler and Alison White. For many years I was based at St Thomas' in Huddersfield. The incumbent at the time, Richard Giles, was a wonderful friend and inspiration. All these people and many others have shaped my understanding of ministry.

Then there are the bishops that I have worked alongside more recently. It was Richard Harries who first invited me to become a bishop and I am hugely grateful for his belief in me and affirmation. My episcopal colleagues in the Chelmsford Diocese have been massively supportive. The sermon at the end of this book was preached at the ordination of my colleague John Wraw, Bishop of Bradwell from 2011 to 2017. His premature death was a tragic loss, but the inspiration of his ministry in the months before he died has blessed me hugely.

I have learned a lot from friends in the episcopal cell group I am part of, especially my dear friend Stephen Conway, the Bishop of Ely, and the much-missed Michael Perham. He and I were ordained bishop alongside each other and shared much about the meaning of practice of ministry.

As I noted earlier, the idea for writing a book on priesthood emerged out of frustration with many of the works that were usually offered to ordinands and I started preparing my annual ordination charges with a view to putting them together into a book at some point. In the Chelmsford Diocese we have been wonderfully blessed by those who have served us as Directors of Ordinands. They have also supported this project and I want to thank Philip Need, our current DDO, in particular. I asked him and my colleague Roger Matthews and also Sue Rose, the DDO for Bath and Wells Diocese, to read the manuscript in draft. Their encouraging, incisive, pertinent and sometimes critical comments have enormously improved the book.

While writing the book I did an MA in Christian Leadership though St Mellitus College and Middlesex University. For my dissertation I wrote about the word 'sentinel', its significance for Christian ministry and its neglect in most things written on the subject. This book, I hope, begins to redress that balance. I am very grateful to the staff at St Mellitus College for their support, especially Graham Tomlin, Andy Emerton, Jane Williams and Sean Doherty. I also spent a couple of weeks at Sarum College researching some of the background to the book. James Woodward, the Principal, made me wonderfully welcome and was a great encourager.

I also want to record my thanks to Katherine Venn, my commissioning editor, and all the team at Hodder & Stoughton for their support of this project.

Finally, I am hugely grateful to all the ordinands I have worked with and had the privilege of ordaining. This book is dedicated to them and through them to all the people they serve. The refining fire of their questions, their eagerness to learn and their willingness to serve have been the greatest inspiration and education of all.

NOTES

Introduction

1 Seamus Heaney, *Station Island* (Faber & Faber Ltd, 1984), p. 89. Used by permission.

Chapter 1 *Priests for a priestly people*

1 *Common Worship, Ordination Services* (Church House Publishing, 2007), p. 55. This explanation of ministry gathers together key scriptural texts from 1 Peter 2.9–10 and 1 Corinthians 12.27; 3.16.

2 ibid., p. 4.

3 Nicholas Henshall, from the extended epilogue to his father's book, *Dear Nicholas: A Father's Letter to his Newly Ordained Son*, by Michael Henshall (Sacristy Press, 2019), pp. 35–6.

4 *Common Worship, Ordination Services*, p. 31.

5 ibid., p. 55.

6 ibid. and based on 1 Timothy 6.20.

7 ibid., p. 32.

8 ibid.

9 ibid., p. 37.

10 ibid., p. 55.

11 ibid., p. 37.

12 Actually the Ordinal uses the word 'watchman', but for all sorts of reasons, not least the preferability of inclusive language wherever possible, the word 'sentinel' appears to me to be richer and more appropriate.

13 There is some evidence to suggest ordination rites were being used as early as the consecration of Robert Ferrar as Bishop of St David's in September 1548, but this is not certain, and anyway, in this time of religious, and therefore liturgical, upheaval, various texts may well have been produced and experiments in liturgy undertaken. See Paul F. Bradshaw, *The Anglican Ordinal: Its History and Development from the*

Reformation to the Present Day (SPCK/Alcuin Club, 1971), pp. 18–36.

14 On such a sensitive and significant issue – the very identity of ministry – Cranmer and his supporters had been reluctant to face down the conservative bishops who still opposed his liturgical reforms. He decided to keep his liturgical powder dry until the balance of senior bishops was in favour of his developments. See Diarmaid MacCulloch, *Thomas Cranmer: A Life* (Yale University Press, 1996), pp. 397 and 460.

15 Alternative Service Book (SPCK, 1980), p. 356.

16 *The Book of Common Prayer: The Texts of 1549, 1559, and 1662*, edited with Introduction and Notes by Brian Cummings (Oxford University Press, 2011), p. 636.

17 Frank Senn, *Christian Liturgy; Catholic and Evangelical* (Fortress Press, 1997), p. 369.

18 Howard Dellar, http://archive.churchsociety.org/churchman/documents/Cman_106_4_Dellar.pdf. Accessed 19 April 2017.

19 Paul F. Bradshaw, 'A Brief History of Ordination Rites', in *Common Worship, Ordination Services Study Edition* (Church House Publishing, 2007), pp. 118–19.

20 *Didache*, 15.2.

21 Hippolytus, *On the Apostolic Tradition*, English version with Introduction and Commentary by Alistair Stewart-Sykes (St Vladimir's Seminary Press, 2001), p. 61.

22 Consequently I wrote my MA dissertation on *Why the Ordinal of the Church of England Describes Priests as Sentinels, and Why it Matters*. It is available on request.

23 Even books like Paul Bradshaw's *The Anglican Ordinal* or Colin Buchanan's *Modern Anglican Ordination Rites* (Grove Liturgical Study 51, 1987), while being extremely helpful in every other respect, focus on the history and development of the Ordination Prayer and do not deal with the Declaration in any detail at all.

24 MacCulloch, *Thomas Cranmer*, p. 461. Moreover, in one of his treatises Cranmer wrote: 'If they are to be loved, honoured and esteemed that be the King's chancellors, judges, officers and ministers in temporal matters; how much then are they to be esteemed that be ministers of Christ's words and sacraments' (Cranmer, *Defence*, p. 456).

25 See the current anxieties over the interchangeability of Methodist and Anglican presbyteral ministry, all of which rests on different theologies

of episcopacy and the particularity of episcopal ordination.

26 This rite has undoubtedly been very influential in the development of ordination rites in the churches of the Reformation and in wider ecumenical dialogue. For further discussion of this and other modern ordination rites see Paul F. Bradshaw, *Rites of Ordination: Their History and Theology* (SPCK, 2014), pp. 191–213.

27 D.E.W. Harrison and Michael C. Sansom, *Worship in the Church of England* (SPCK, 1982), p. 173.

28 R.C.D. Jasper, *The Development of the Anglican Liturgy 1662–1980* (SPCK, 1989), pp. 331–4.

29 'Every effort has been made in ASB to provide a set of services which would not only place no obstacle in the way of Roman Catholic recognition of Anglican Orders but also give consideration to the views of the Free Churches on the ministry' wrote R.C.D. Jasper in *A New Dictionary of Liturgy and Worship*, ed. J.G. Davies (SCM Press, 1986), pp. 405.

30 *Common Worship, Ordination Services*, p. 39.

31 ibid.

32 This Declaration affirms that the Church of England is part of the One, Holy, Catholic and Apostolic Church, worshipping the one true God, Father, Son and Holy Spirit, and professing faith that is uniquely revealed in the Holy Scriptures and set out in the Catholic Creeds, that is, the Apostles Creed, the Nicene Creed and the Athanasian Creed. It goes on to affirm that these truths are carried by the Church of England's historic formularies, the Thirty-Nine Articles of Religion, the Book of Common Prayer and the Ordering of Bishops, Priests and Deacons. In ecumenical discussion this Declaration of Assent is a document that is often referred to. It places the Church of England and its formularies within the historic flow of Christian witness. We note that the Ordinal is part of that.

33 *Common Worship, Ordination Services*, p. 31.

Chapter 2   *Servant*

1 *Common Worship, Ordination Services*, p. 10.

2 ibid., p. 37.

3 ibid., p. 10.

4 ibid., p. 15.

Chapter 3 Shepherd

1 These references are often negative: the prophets criticise those who should shepherd God's people more faithfully. Nevertheless, this shows how potent and widespread the image was. See, for instance, Jeremiah 23.2–4 or Ezekiel 34.2–8.

2 See *With the Smell of the Sheep: Pope Francis Speaks to Priests, Bishops and Other Shepherds* (Orbis, 2017).

3 *Common Worship, Ordination Services*, p. 32.

4 Augustine, Sermon 46.30 on 'Christ as the One True Shepherd' in *The Works of St Augustine*, trans Edmund Hill, O.P., Part 3, Volumes 1–2 (New City Press, 1999–2009).

5 Augustine, Sermon 339.4 in ibid.

6 St Ambrose of Milan, *On the Duties of the Clergy*, trans Ivor J. Davidson, Oxford Early Christian Studies (Oxford University Press, 2002), 2.41 and 2.60.

7 Though it is good to note that the latest criteria for selection being produced by the Ministry Council of the Church of England is much more aware of these creative differences.

8 https://luminarypodcasts.com/listen/russell-brand-395/under-the-skin-with-russell-brand-luminary-exclusive/83-god-or-no-god-whats-it-to-be-with-bishop-stephen-cottrell/7c475ec2-d5da-47e1-ac96-60e0319c56cc.

9 Marilynne Robinson, *Gilead* (Virago, 2004), p. 275.

10 Roger Morris, sermon preached at Chelmsford Cathedral, 18 April 2019.

11 Robinson, *Gilead*, pp. 183–4.

Chapter 4 Messenger

1 *Common Worship, Ordination Services*, p. 37.

2 Gregory the Great, *Pastoral Rule* (Limovia.Net, 2013), 2.2.

3 These are courses for those wanting to find out about Christian faith and are readily available online and in Christian bookshops.

4 Although it is right and proper for the clergy to take a lead here, increasingly in the Church of England we are seeing many dioceses renewing Reader ministry (itself an important diaconal ministry of the Church), so a theologically trained and licensed lay minister takes responsibility for catechesis in the local church. It is an important and encouraging development.

5   This striking phrase is one we use a lot in the Chelmsford Diocese. It comes from the Lambeth Conference declaration of 1988, stating that 'unless Christians are encouraged to "go to school" with Christ, to be nourished by his teaching and sacraments, and to grow into his likeness (Ephesians 4.11–16) they cannot bear the fruits of discipleship'. This in turn echoes some of the opening lines of the Rule of St Benedict, where he writes: 'And so we are going to establish a school for the service of the Lord.'

6   Lancelot Andrewes, Bishop of Winchester, from 'A Caution before Preaching After the Example of St Fulgentius' in *Preces Privatae*, 1648.

7   Evelyn Underhill, 'Call to the Inner Life', a letter to the Archbishop of Canterbury, Cosmo Gordon Lang, 1931: http://interruptingthesilence. com/2009/06/04/evelyn-underhill-call-to-the-inner-life. Accessed 21 November 2019.

8   *Common Worship, Ordination Services*, p. 44.

Chapter 5   Sentinel

1   *Common Worship, Ordination Services*, p. 37.

2   *The Interpreter's Dictionary of the Bible* (Abingdon Press, 1962), p. 806.

3   For instance, at Romans 13.11 Paul entreats us to 'stay awake', 'to watch'.

4   This text and the way in which Jesus looks into his own Jewish and biblical tradition with a 'sentinel's eye' in order to see and interpret it differently is of missiological and evangelistic significance. On the road, and 'beginning with Moses and all the prophets' Jesus unpacks 'the things about himself in all the scriptures' (Luke 24.27). Something similar takes place every time a preacher breaks open the word in a sermon. The preacher is being a sentinel, looking deeply at the tradition and its relevance for today and listening deeply to the question and concerns of others.

5   *Common Worship*, p. 37.

6   Augustine of Hippo, *Exposition on Psalm 127*, http://www.newadvent. org/fathers/1801127.htm. Accessed 22 April 2017.

7   ibid.

8   ibid. This is a distinctive theme of Augustine's. In his rule for religious communities he wrote of the leader: 'Before you he has to be at your

head in honour; before God, he should be prostrate at your feet in fear', Augustine of Hippo, *The Monastic Rules*, commentary by Gerald Bonner, *The Praeceptum* 7.3 (New City Press, 2004), p. 121.

9   Gregory of Nyssa, *Letter 13*, quoted in Christopher A. Beeley, *Leading God's People: Wisdom from the Early Church for Today* (Eerdmans, 2012), p. 29.

10 ibid.

11 Augustine, *Exposition*.

12 Gregory the Great, 'A Servant of the Servants of God', Homilies on Ezekiel, 1, 11, 4–6 in Robert Atwell, *Spiritual Classics from the Early Church* (Church House Publishing, 1995), p. 183.

13 ibid.

14 Beeley, *Leading God's People*, p. 30.

15 Many spiritual writers and theologians make this point. I read it recently in the first female diocesan bishop in the Anglican Communion's reflection on ministry's perils and opportunities. Speaking of the centrality of contemplative prayer for survival as well as flourishing, she says 'contemplative prayer is the prayer that lets God be God': Penny Jamieson, *Living at the Edge; Sacrament and Solidarity in Leadership* (Mowbray, 1997), p. 188.

16 Coakley is interesting on glossolalia, making connections between the prevalence of tongues in contemporary charismatic spirituality and older contemplative traditions. She quotes Abba Ephraim who said his prayer was sometimes like 'a well bubbling out of his mouth' (*Apopthgegmata Patrum*, Ephraim 2) or the 'disorderly' words of Teresa of Avila saying 'the soul longs to pour out words of praise': *God, Sexuality and the Self: An essay 'On the Trinity'* (Cambridge University Press, 2013), pp. 172–3.

17 Coakley is critical of 'contemplative elitism'. From the twelfth century onwards the Western Church made a distinction 'between "meditation" (discursive reflection on Scripture) and "contemplation" (this more vulnerable activity of "space making")' that wasn't always helpful. The sixteenth-century Carmelites, Teresa of Avila and John of the Cross, for instance, speak about transitioning from meditation to contemplation as if contemplation is better and harder and more advanced: ibid., p. 126.

18 Sarah Coakley, *Powers and Submissions: Spirituality, Philosophy and Gender* (Wiley, 2009), p. 35.

19 Henri Nouwen, *In the Name of Jesus, Reflections on Christian Leadership* (Darton, Longman & Todd, 1989), p. 29.

20 Walter Brueggemann, *The Prophetic Imagination*, Fortress Press, 1978, p. 44.

21 ibid., p. 45.

22 Walter Brueggemann, *Interrupting Silence: God's Command to Speak Out* (Hodder & Stoughton, 2018), p. 1.

23 Rowan Williams, 'The New Evangelisation for the Transmission of the Christian Faith', address to the Thirteenth Ordinary Assembly of the Synod of Bishops, 2012, p. 8: http://cadeio.org/blog/wp-content/uploads/2014/01/Archbishop-Rowan-Williams-Address-to-the-Synod-of-Bishops.pdf. Accessed 11 April 2018.

24 Rowan Williams, *A Silent Action: Engagements with Thomas Merton* (SPCK, 2013), p. 50.

25 *Common Worship, Ordination Services*, p. 37.

26 Jack Nicholls, farewell sermon to Sheffield Diocese, 9 June 2008

27 Rowan Williams, 'The Christian Priest Today', lecture on the occasion of the 150th anniversary of Ripon College, Cuddesdon: http://aoc2013.brix.fatbeehive.com/articles.php/2097/the-christian-priest-today-lecture-on-the-occasion-of-the-150th-anniversary-of-ripon-college-cuddesd. Accessed 12 October 2019.

28 ibid.

29 Brueggemann, *Interrupting Silence*, p. 25.

30 See, for instance, Jeremiah 38.4.

31 Gregory the Great, *Pastoral Rule*, 2.6.

32 Beeley, Leading God's People, p. 43.

33 Gregory the Great, *A Servant of the Servants*, p.183.

34 Don Paterson, 'Why Do You Stay Up So Late?', in *Rain* (Faber & Faber, 2009), p. 9.

35 ibid.

36 *Common Worship Ordination Services*, p. 37.

37 Rowan Williams, 'The Christian Priest Today', 2004.

Chapter 6   Steward

1 *Common Worship, Ordination Services*, p. 37.

2 The Declaration of Assent, in ibid., p. 6.

3 Gregory Nazianzen famously suggested that a priest must be like a

skilled harp player able to play many strings at once. But I think conductor is a better image.

4 *Rites of Ordination of a Bishop, of Priests and of Deacons* (the Roman Pontifical as renewed by decree of the Second Vatican Ecumenical Council published by authority of Pope Paul VI and further revised at the direction of Pope John Paul II): http://ordination. ceegee.org/rite.pdf. Accessed 12 October 2019.

5 Quoted in Kenneth Leech, *Spirituality and Pastoral Care* (Sheldon Press, 1986), p. 131.

6 Don't be put off by the different words the Church uses to describe the one service of Holy Communion. The term 'holy communion' emphasises our intimacy with God when we share bread and wine. The word 'eucharist' means thanksgiving, and highlights holy communion as the great prayer and thanksgiving of the Church. The word 'mass' comes from the final words of the Latin mass, *Ite, missa est,* meaning 'go' and emphasises holy communion as rations of the journey of life. The words 'mass' and 'mission' are really one and the same. They are about the apostolic vocation of the Church. Different parts of the Church tend to use different words. We should love all of them.

7 Cummings (ed.), *The Book of Common Prayer: The Texts*, p. 402.

8 *Common Worship, Ordination Services*, p. 43.

9 ibid.

10 ibid., p. 39.

11 ibid.

12 ibid.

13 Nouwen, *In the Name of Jesus*, p. 64.

Chapter 7   *Carrying the cross*

1 *Common Worship, Ordination Services*, p. 32.

Chapter 8   *Guarding the heart*

1 Rowan Williams, *Being Christian* (SPCK, 2014), pp. 57–8.

2 What I have also learned is that he was consciously misquoting Julian of Norwich who said, 'Thou shalt rest and thou shalt pray.'

3 *Common Worship, Ordination Services*, p. 38.

4 I have written about this aspect of leadership in much greater depth